Ears

LEHEL VANDOR

Copyright © 2008, 2014 by Lehel Vandor

Second Editions, Revised & Updated

Originally published in the United Kingdom in 2008 by YouWriteOn & Legend Press.

Cover: Photo of Tirgu Mures town centre (1990) Copyright © by Lehel Vandor; processed portrait of Nicolae Ceausescu, Cover Design Copyright © by Lehel Vandor

All rights reserved.

ISBN: 1502723417
ISBN-13: 978-1502723413

DEDICATION

To my Mother, for getting me hooked on beautiful words, sounds, and pictures, which were my solid shelters during many storms.

CONTENTS

I.	PORTRAIT	1
II.	HOME	6
III.	LIGHT	10
IV.	CONCRETE	17
V.	HEAT	24
VI.	PRAISE	29
VII.	METAL	33
VIII.	SCHOOL	40
IX.	FOOD	47
X.	SOUL	52
XI.	REALM	59
XII.	BREATH	64
XIII.	VISION	74
XIV.	DREAM	79
XV.	REVOLUTION	83
XVI.	POWER	96

XVII.	MONEY	106
XVIII.	EXCHANGE	119
XIX.	EXPERIMENT	126
XX.	ETHER	133
XXI.	EVOLUTION	139
XXII.	CHOICE	153

I. PORTRAIT

At first, there was one ear.

Just one, due to laws of optics that not even the absolute powers of the Leader could alter. One visible ear attached to a well-known and ubiquitous face; a face immortalised by a photographer from a semi-frontal viewpoint, which rendered the portrait benevolent, almost fatherly.

It was *the* portrait, hung on the wall in every office and in every classroom... It hovered with a fatherly smile in the peripheral vision of pupils who stared at the mostly terrestrial, sometimes hellish, and very rarely heavenly things that used to unfold on the blackboard.

The same portrait smiled at us when we opened any of our battered and almost disintegrating schoolbooks... Those books were handed to us, at the start of each school year, in a storeroom that was filled with huge piles of amorphous-looking cellulose. It was a room where the smell of mould and rot in our very young minds created the mental image of something that was not a fountain, but rather a very old well of knowledge.

One of our key tasks, as soon as we got our hands on the schoolbooks, was to check very carefully that the portrait was intact. Had anybody drawn anything on it during the book's previous autumn-to-summer lifecycle, during which the book had been spreading spores of knowledge mixed with ideologically altered lies? Had it been altered later, during its summer hibernation, in the mouldy storage areas? Had it been damaged or torn? Or, Heaven forbid, had someone removed it?

One had to report any anomaly immediately, in order to avoid accusations of subversive vandalism, which always had scary consequences.

Then, after a summer that we had again spent near a stoic river, far from dangerous ears, under a sky packed with ideology-free sunshine, came a very memorable autumn... The mouldy and smelly room, the source of the new school year's worries and revelations, greeted us with heaps of previously unimaginable surprises.

Some schoolbooks were new; others had survived their usual summer hibernation as collections of pages held together only by the cohesion force between the thoughts expressed on them - but all the books of that special autumn contained a change, which was beyond our wildest imagination.

The previously untouchable and unalterable portraits had changed in the smaller heap of new books. In the old books, the portraits had been changed by an act of cosmic proportions: something had ripped out the old portraits, and then replaced them with new ones, which were glued to the front page.

The new portraits were showing *two* ears.

Two ears, on a full-frontal portrait of an alien-looking creature - the result of a new photo shoot that occurred twenty-odd years after the previous picture. It was the result of photochemical processes that could only depict a much-aged man in front of the lens, and of a heavy, overdone retouching job.

It represented an artificial perfection, which *had* to have, obviously, ears that were no longer obscured by the laws of optics. The monumental cost of reprints, replacements of zillions of portraits in every possible size on the walls and in books did not matter. It showed unequivocally just how strong bionic arms could the regime flex, whenever it wished to alter appearances.

The legend goes that the Leader was told by someone in his entourage that his previous portrait had been imperfect... because of those darn subversive laws of optics.

From a distance that does not reveal the heavy, bizarre retouching, behold - a flawless portrait of a flawless man, the immaculate Leader, who had shaped and would forever shape an equally flawless model society.

It had one more ear, for overhearing dangerous thoughts voiced by careless, unsuspecting lips; it also illustrated the desperate strive for the sustaining of a fake image of a darker reality...

While I was remembering the unexpected metamorphosis of that portrait, countless other memories and images flooded my mind. However, memoirs are usually written by people who go through rustling bundles of sepia-toned images and yellow, stained pages of the mind... before that treasure chest terminally decays together with the valuable, fading relics it had been keeping for many years.

Then there are people with memories that, after a while, start to seem like acquired collections of someone *else*'s surreal celluloid strips, film cells seen at some point in the past and now rapidly fading - a decay hastened by the clash between their very absurdity and the rational mind's immune reaction. That mind, instead of blocking them out, just mellows all those irrationalities and all that absurdity into a bundle of seemingly second-hand, indirect experiences.

The world that surrounded me during the first nineteen years of my life, a world shaped by Ceausescu's regime of daily Kafkaesque assault on rational thought, has been radically changing since the Christmas of 1989.

There have been many volumes written about such societies, countless hours filled with documentaries on the vast political, economical and of course, ideological forces at work... The following recollections though, from the Romanian pre-

and post-Revolutionary years, are street-level snapshots with often-surprising similarities between the old and the new country.

They come together not as a grand portal into the past and quasi-present, but a small window for just one head at a time to peer through it.

These are my film cells, my cut-up, fading film strips... projected for the first time in a continuous passing through the personal chest of relics, just when I am about to truly begin to believe that these are just somebody else's visions seen in a cinema I have never been in, made by a cinematographer who never existed.

After I had left that country almost twenty years ago, I regularly returning there to this day; there, I can still meet and converse with many ghosts who cosily nest in the altered, and recently turned ultra-materialistic, world of the Carpathian Mountains.

This book is about the past in which those ghosts still possessed powerful bodies in my weathered homeland, making Europe seem just some distant mirage; it is also about the present in which that world, still silently and slowly being kneaded by these ghosts, has hastily re-decorated its façade for the suddenly so reachable and tangible Europe...

My homeland has been copying the West indiscriminately, eagerly, and *desperately*. While it is copying, in every respect, the world that has become my new home, latter seems to have been gradually permeated by thoughts that I was hoping to leave behind in terms of both time and space. The eerie resurrection of totalitarian concepts and violations of basic human liberties in the citadel of democracy in which I live in, all committed in the name of building a "safer" society, were terrifying for someone who had seen the very same thoughts and strategies in action - albeit in a very different world.

During the regime, we had been having just one major fear in our everyday lives; later, as we began to copy the West, we have successfully created a new way of life in which we have the hard-earned freedom to choose between many new fears...

We are as fearful of calories, germs, wrinkles, and interest rates as the world that we are copying is.

Still, my former home is a place of pilgrimage where I go to re-charge my emotional batteries. It is a world where, despite the still dire economic situation and everyday hardships, people have not yet forgotten how to be human and humane. That place of pilgrimage is also one that, to this day, reminds me of just how much good and how much evil people are capable of.

Seeing shades of that evil emerging in the West under different colours and façades is an experience I was not expecting. I was able to follow how one society was desperately trying to deny the existence of its sinister ghosts, while another was happy to invoke them as cures for its new problems.

While I was gathering courage, and ended up embarking on this rather lexical voyage, I realised how much I owe all those close-by and remote voices, columnists, writers and "ordinary people" who managed to capture, and still have a brilliant grasp on, the many facets of past and present realities. They are doing this without having lost their sense of proportion or their reference points in the maelstrom of still ongoing changes.

II. HOME

My hometown, Marosvásárhely (or Tirgu Mures in Romanian), is one of the medieval cities that are scattered between the mountains that surround Transylvania.

It comfortably rests in the valley of the river Maros, in just one of the many valleys that spread themselves on the map like half-open protecting hands... Often, these valleys had not been protective enough, but at least they had been able to soften the sounds of thunderstorms and of much too numerous battles into a gentle rumble, which had reverberated along the many rivers of that bruised land...

During peacetime, my hometown used to gaze down on lively markets that were unfolding their tents on the plains that lay outside its old fortified walls... hence the city acquired its name, which means marketplace on river Maros...

It had seen very turbulent and often blood-red waters flow from the mountains, pass under its walls... Between contemplative rests that it had managed to spend by the river, it had endured many unpredictable, howling storms, which had been brought to that valley by both Nature and Man over the centuries...

The old city walls are still standing on those hills, layers of the more recent past are expanding around them in all directions. The multi-coloured mix of stones, bricks and concrete had flown from those heights, like some artificial lava flow that had spread and changed over many centuries and many miles.

Some parts of that flow coagulated into a glorious historical city centre... and, having left there most of its colours, the remaining grey concrete flow continued further down, followed the river Maros, gradually aged and sedimented into monochrome deserts of communist blocks of flats... Then, just before it completely settled, its edges finally solidified into the shape of a monstrous chemical plant on the edge of the city. Beyond that, untouched green land lies next to the river; the two of them are reminiscing about the more distant centuries, which only they can remember.

The house in which I grew up in is on the edge of the historic city centre. Since the 1840s, it has endured all the regimes and changes that history has brought. It still comfortably rests its back against a steep hill. Acacia trees grow on the slope of that hill; their dizzying scent has been gently rolling downhill into our courtyard.

At just a few minutes' walking distance from there, in a place where suddenly the multicoloured noise of the city changes to green stillness, the all-muscle river that rushes down from the mountains is being lulled and hushed by the great water lock that protects the city.

All this sits pretty much right in the middle of Transylvania where, unlike vampires, eminently non-fictional creatures had been spilling and consuming blood for too many centuries.

They had been doing this in broad daylight, immune to garlic; they had been casting onto those hills and plains of ever-changing colour very long and very dense shadows that persist to this day in political life, in the ethnic tensions arising from the echoes of annexing this former Hungarian territory to Romania... These shadows are also present in the collective psyche, which a quarter of a century ago freed itself from the most recent non-fictional, demented, but very calculated, Evil.

I grew up there, during Ceausescu's so-called Golden Era...

I cannot recall whether there was one certain moment when I realised that everything that had surrounded me had been an absurd play set in a tiny, claustrophobia-inducing theatre.

I still find it difficult to reconcile those two sides of me... One side is that small kid who was opening his eyes and ears tentatively and, initially, very fearfully; a happy kid who was maximally enjoying a truly minimalist childhood, who was accepting the food rationing and power cuts, propaganda and fake celebrations as normal, and the one and only possible, reality. Then there is that other person, the grown-up, who is looking back, finding that reality a weird one that is filled with funny and sad absurdities.

There is also the dilemma that Krzysztof Kieslowski wrote so eloquently about... What do I consider home? Where do I feel at home?

Transylvania is still criss-crossed by as many ethnic tensions exploited in everyday and political life as many mountain streams it possesses, hence it makes one feel discriminated against. Hungary, the land of my mother tongue, has had enough of tidal waves of Transylvanian Hungarian immigrants, so it does not quite look at them with fondness. It gave them the possibility to obtain Hungarian citizenship; however, ordinary people there still look at the Transylvanian Hungarians as people who are primarily economic migrants. Then, there is Great Britain, infused with very familiar-sounding, extreme and xenophobic thoughts, partial truths and astounding distortions that are coming from certain major parties. Latter are gaining more and more support, whenever the emotional (and always irrational) buttons about immigration are pressed in order to gain some political advantage.

In the end, the answer to the question that Kieslowski posed is actually quite simple...

I still go *home* when I fly to that bruised land surrounded by mountains. I still only feel at home among those people whom I share common experiences with – people, who had not forgotten how to be human even during extremely inhuman times.

III. LIGHT

Schooldays arrived in my life well after I had learnt the fundamental physics of light and heat. Of course, I had not understood by then their complex laws - but I certainly knew how ideological darkness and cold political calculation could fundamentally affect them in my everyday life.

Due to shortages in classrooms, we were doing 'afternoon shifts' on certain weeks, whilst during normal weeks we used to start school at 8AM... Each day the joyous, and often luminous, games of the mind that filled the hours spent in the school were quite different from what used to come after school.

I used to find my way home on streets that were rendered pitch black by power saving measures introduced by the Party. The streets between my school and my home were just constellations of warm orange, yellow, and reddish flecks of lights, which were seeping through the curtains of myriad windows, originating from petroleum lamps, candles, and battery-powered torches. These sometimes projected on the curtains the shadows of tired bodies animated by even more tired souls.

The economics of these regular and long power cuts never made any sense, because the energy consumption of the general population was infinitesimal when compared to what old-fashioned and hopelessly obsolete industrial monsters were devouring. For example, the aluminium plant at *Slatina* was making deplorable quality aluminium via an old electrolysis method, soaking up every electron that the also terribly inefficient old power plants around it could squeeze out of low-grade coal or methane.

Therefore, there was no point in doing calculations about the economics of our blackouts... but these power cuts, during which the flames of a petroleum lamp in the kitchen were projecting our quivering shadows onto our walls and curtains, were meant to make us very aware of the powers that governed our reality.

Darkness, physical or mental, is a powerful tool – especially when both kinds are combined...

I was lucky to live a mere fifteen minutes' walk away from my first school, and this manageable distance shrunk as my tiny legs grew.

Only half of this daily journey consisted of a dreary walk on dark streets, where I always lost my shadow - like a true Transylvanian creature of the night. Still, from those dark streets I could always see in the distance an oasis of light: just one part of one street, which always stayed immune to the exasperatingly regular power cuts.

The small oasis of light that I used to encounter every day on my way home happened to be on our street. The oasis did not quite reach as far as our house, but it still allowed me on every winter afternoon a glorious transition from darkness decorated by coloured specks of light to a cosy, yellow world lit by sodium vapour streetlights.

After that oasis, came a transition back to the darkness in which I used to reach our house.

I used to find my mother immersed in the silent joy of crossword puzzles, near a petroleum lamp in the kitchen, always waiting for me, always ready to serve a tasty, hot meal cooked with glorious imagination from desperately simple ingredients.

The reason for the existence of that small and very rare oasis of electrical bliss on our street, an oasis where my shadow used to return for a while, was a non-stop bread factory.

As we had to stand in huge queues for our daily bread rations, we never managed to figure out where that factory's output was disappearing to, but that grey temple of beautiful smells possessed its own power line. Somehow, that power line, which had been giving the factory its vital juice, was not separated from the circuits that used to supply electricity to a few dozen houses and streetlights around it...

The mighty flows of electrons used to return to our homes eventually, just before the evening TV programs.

We were treated to three hours of TV per day on two national channels that were carried over the Carpathian Mountains by a few relay stations. Without their help, the TV programmes would not have been able to cross the mountains and to bring into our home that Voice and that Face...

However, as he had done so countless times during history, Man managed to spill his evil over mountain peaks – but this time round his dark emissaries were riding on electromagnetic waves, which were reaching every corner of Transylvania, every day, after too many hours of hissing, grey static...

Those three hours were mostly filled by a tedious, but always victorious, newsreel that showed that day's amazing achievements... Then a program of made-up pseudo-folk music and dance used to follow; this alternated with odes and hymns, which had special lyrics praising the glory of the Party...

However, usually once a week, there was some TV moment about *something*. A play. A fragment of a classical recital that was filmed somewhere. Rarely, some imported joy - maybe an old Thames Television play with (so they thought...) ideologically safe Shakespeare. Sometimes, they aired some foreign science program about the future, about technology - a future that, of course, would arrive a lot sooner in the glorious society we were building...

The TV schedule used to stretch to an awesome five or mind-blowing six hours on Saturday afternoons, and two long chunks on Sunday. These, too were of course mostly filled with propaganda and folk music — but they aired some carefully filtered glimpses into that vast world that was hiding beyond the Iron Curtain.

The classic trick that they used in order to make us sit in front of the propaganda shows, even if we never actively watched them, was to announce the screening of a film. They usually cut it in half, with a second part that was to follow at some point later. The first part usually aired as scheduled, but then we had to sit and wait during grossly over-run propaganda shows, hoping and hoping — just to find out much later that the second part was cancelled.

It was then rescheduled, and often cancelled again on the following week. Eventually it was aired of course; otherwise, the bait would not have worked after a few months of such manipulative fun. I still recall how I managed to watch, for the first time in my life, *Gone with the Wind*, stretched over a three-month period in short chunks - as if they were body parts torn apart by the gusts of communist propaganda.

Oh, but we also had TV series like *Dallas*, because anything that showed the decadence of the West was deemed educational. Thus, while we were trying to forget about our monthly food rations and daily power cuts, we could watch, and empathise with, Miss Ellie Ewing. Poor old woman was being torn by a terrible dilemma: whether she should drill on her husband's land, ignoring the old man's dying wishes or... maybe make some extra millions of dollars from the oil she was expecting to find there. Obviously, we could so identify with such dilemmas...

But... there was also radio.

It truly *was* magic... with its countless channels of radio waves that were bouncing off the ionosphere, all carrying on their invisible and undulating shoulders messages from distant lands... All those waves were being transformed by our ancient valve radio into allowed, or much forbidden, sounds and words.

Later we bought a sturdy, indestructible and so-called portable transistor radio, which was packed full of the super-dense neutron star material of Soviet engineering. It was indeed portable, if one possessed decent muscles - since it was over-engineered to survive maybe even blasts from imperialist missiles...

My father once managed to knock this VEF206 radio down from the top of the fridge... Of course, the black plastic skin was smashed to bits, but the radio's massive endoskeleton stayed intact with all the electronics inside it. With stoicism, which was in sharp contrast with our panic that unfolded around its shattered body, it continued to croon. Later we glued together the plastic bits, and this gave the radio a rather strange shape...

Those boxes of magic sounds were keeping us entertained for many years. Most of the time we tuned in to the few channels that managed to cross the border between the more liberal Hungary and our homeland. We used to listen to these particular stations because they were in Hungarian, my oppressed mother tongue - but also because they were talking openly about things we could not bring up in a public conversation.

Radio Kossuth, a station named after the great Hungarian, used to bring into our home radio plays and political satire that was way beyond anything we could have said on our streets infested with opportunistic informers.

Whenever we craved seriously dangerous thoughts, we tuned in to *Voice of America* and *Radio Free Europe*; both used to broadcast in Hungarian and Romanian languages. Their precious waves were always fading in and out, occasionally perturbed by jamming stations that, ironically, seemed to be hampered by the geological realities of Transylvania, so they never operated well enough. Being reported for listening to these stations meant serious trouble.

Via these radio stations, we could hear from dissidents who had escaped our world and had settled in various other worlds where, as we used to believe, freedom was as normal and abundant as air was. We also heard about events we did not know about, due to local media blackouts.

Such news and thoughts, from thousands of miles away, used to help us get a better picture on our local reality…

My uncle, who lived in a block of flats, had to listen to his VEF206 radio at very low volume, just to make sure that the heresies carried into the small flat by unstoppable waves of the ether could not be heard through the thin walls. The small, battery-operated and ultra-heavy VEF206 transistor radio had become the most valuable object in our house. With its sounds, it managed to paint vivid tableaus that our TV set, connected to an aerial that could only receive national TV channels, could not.

Later, toward the end of the 1980s (and the end of *that* world), analogue satellite receivers were smuggled in. Small companies began to manufacture satellite dishes, and for many people this meant that their field of view onto the outside world radically widened. Many, like our family, could not afford the 'imported' gizmos, so we invented ways of peeking through the same electronic window that others had installed in their homes.

Such peeking only necessitated a well-calculated simple antenna aimed at some neighbour's satellite receiver. It managed to capture faint, wobbly images from the already demodulated TV-band signals, which used to escape from the analogue tuner boxes. The resulting images were sometimes with sound, often without, and were always conditioned by what the others were watching and when… In blocks of flats, neighbours often agreed between them to share the costs and they split the signal into several flats; they used to agree with the owner of the receiver what to watch.

We installed our concoction in the loft of our house, and aimed it at a neighbour's house *vis-à-vis*. Later on my first cousin, whom we shared the courtyard with, installed his own satellite dish and tuner in our loft, via the good old who-knows-who network and some extra money he decided to sacrifice. Whenever they left for the weekend to visit the wife's parents in a nearby village, my cousin used to leave the tuner turned on for us - and then we had two days of continuous satellite TV heaven.

We were lucky (again...) that the satellite dish was not visible from outside the house. This proved to be important, because in the autumn of 1989, just months before the regime's glorious and overblown hot air balloon took a fatal puncture wound, the regime had decided to make satellite equipments illegal.

They simply wanted to close that enormous electronic window, which offered sweeping vistas onto an enormous world out there, beyond the Iron Curtain. Police began to knock on people's doors, enforced the new measures that had been born, like everything else during those final days, out of chemically pure paranoia. None of that really mattered any more, though... as we found out not much later, when December 1989 arrived.

.

IV. CONCRETE

While the regime was physically starving the population, it was obsessively spending on huge building projects: palaces for the Party's elite, monuments and symbols of communist supremacy – and vast numbers of blocks of flats. Countless old, sometimes even historic, but far from crumbling houses were replaced with bland, stacked, impersonal boxes of concrete.

In every city, the demolitions were advancing on mysterious and unpredictable routes, like some waves of sand and dust blown around by the winds of communist megalomania. The same strange winds were uprooting the inhabitants of those old houses, depositing them in newly built grey boxes.

Large areas of my hometown gradually disappeared; they were devoured by the bionic, huffing and puffing, brick eating, and rectangular monotony-excreting monsters... Even historic buildings were just plain food for that monster, unless they happened to be listed monuments. Sometimes, the beast glanced at some cluster of houses that were trembling in its shadow, it turned toward them – but then it changed its mind because of some chaotic bureaucratic processes that were taking place in its strange mind. Thus, for some reason, it let those houses alone.

Our historic city centre mostly managed to evade the rapid advances of the new, the bad, and the ugly. Other cities and towns were not so fortunate - especially not in Transylvania, where an extra political agenda existed. Buildings of the past were, well, Hungarian buildings of a Hungarian past - so it was even more important to erase those.

Ironically, the regime did not spare quintessentially Romanian cities, either... Even Bucharest, a city that had been known in the 1930s as "the little Paris" due to its charming, atmospheric streets and the many palaces of the Romanian aristocracy, was mostly turned into a grey pattern.

Our house survived several such onslaughts of communist megalomania... and then, just when the edge of the seemingly unstoppably expanding concrete desert reached one end of our street, the regime ended. We had already received the plans from the authorities that told us the dates of our relocation, and my parents were planning for the move - but then history suddenly intervened in December 1989.

If a house was a nationalised one, then its former owners or the current occupiers were given a much shorter notice period, and they were relocated to the concrete wastelands. However, if the house was privately owned by its occupiers, then they benefited from a longer notice period and a rather symbolic monetary compensation, which was quite laughable.

When I was twelve, a dear old woman began to teach me English that was as elegant as she was. She taught me a language that was very different to the concrete monotony in which she lived.

Together with her two sisters, she was a direct descendant of the grand *Zichy* family of counts. Unlike her sisters, she had decided to remain in Transylvania – so, the communists took everything from her when they came to power. She kept writing much-censored letters to her sisters who after the Second World War had sensed the approach of an even greater and longer lasting storm and had fled to France and Germany.

She spoke several languages fluently; she quoted the classics in original. In her tiny apartment, she was guarding her precious old books that somehow had not been taken by that great and destructive storm, wonderful books that had survived the raids of many different monsters.

My awareness of what was hiding under the grey camouflage of Ceausescu's expanding concrete deserts was growing daily. Hence, back then I often wondered what she had felt during all that transition, that slowly advancing cancer that was devouring everything. What was it like to have come from a beautiful past I could not imagine, and then land in that claustrophobic new reality?

The forced nomads of the Socialist glory continued their lives in the new concrete boxes. Their homes with large rooms, tall ceilings, spacious courtyards or gardens, and cosy terracotta stoves had imploded into a few square metres of centrally heated (or almost-warmed) spaces. Thus, the moving of one's gorgeous antique furniture into these new "homes" was a utopia. The new nomads had to sell their invariably beautiful furniture, and bought new ones made of sawdust.

The bookshelves were the funniest ones. They bent and failed as soon as one put a few books on them; the side panels used to bulge when humid weather came, then creaked and bent into avant-garde shapes when dry heat came...

My uncle, who was moved with his family into a flat on the tenth floor, had cupboards and wardrobes that used to amuse me as a kid. The sound that their doors were making (oh, if H. P. Lovecraft could have heard them!), and the amount of force needed to open or close them, continuously changed with the weather. Depending on the amount of humidity, the bent surfaces of the furniture were rubbing against other bent surfaces...

Lifts were only occasionally in working order in these towering pinnacles of communist architecture. Even when the lifts did work, they often needed certain special human assistance. A finger, pressed against a sensor or an electrical contact... A human body, leaning on the door or on some metallic panel, pressing something out of (or into?) shape, making some wiring work finally...

Usually, the lights in the lift did not work, because people were regularly stealing the neon tube or the light bulb. Therefore, before the days of sensuous LCD panels and seductive backlit buttons in the lifts, we used to rely on approximate pokes in the dark until we ended up on the right floor. Who could have possibly complained that visiting anyone in such a block of flats was boring?

The blocks of flats were often numbered in the most chaotic fashion. Parts of the number sequence stopped, continued orthogonally on a different street's other side, then disappeared, re-surfaced further on, continued along another route, and looped back eventually to the street it started on. Many of those numbering schemes survive to the present day, and cabbies with a pinch of masochistic inclination can still find them quite interesting.

Ceausescu's well-documented homogenisation policy was by no means original, and it was ethnically motivated - it involved the moving of tens of thousands of families from the South and the East of Romania to Transylvania. On one hand, it diluted the local ethnic minority communities. On the other hand, it had many non-numeric effects: if one moves so many people to an area that they do not know its history of, or anything about its culture, then one also dilutes those local characteristics and they gradually vanish.

As a kid, I used to cross a part of the city that was purpose-built for these migrants of the regime's so-called Golden Era. There, I could observe first-hand how their customs and ways of life had been grafted onto the urban landscape in sometimes downright hilarious ways.

Some of these people had installed a horseshoe workshop on the first floor of a block of flats... When a horse made a sound above my head, I had a mild shock, which soon turned into paralysing fits of laughter. They also planted and cultivated vegetables in the rooms, after they had replaced the flooring with soil; flats on the floor below always ended up with water leaking through the ceiling...

Such homogenisation led to dark overtones, when these

people started to make remarks on how Hungarian ethnics were from barbaric tribes who arrived to an ancient Romanian land. We used to say, "Yes, we did arrive there, but we came on horseback – and not on trains…"

Such tensions generated extremism on both sides; they caused politically exploited distortions of historic facts, generated mass delusions. Many such distortions survive to this day and continue to be exploited in local and national politics. The parallels with current takes on multi-culturalism, political correctness, and immigration issues are remarkably obvious.

By the time I went to school, my parents had renovated one of the rooms of our house. It became my study room, and my successfully inherited obsession with books demanded extra bookshelves. We bought some, similar to the ones those forced into block flats could buy - and behind each row of books, my Dad had to put little sticks that propped up the back of the shelves in order to stop them from bending under the weight. Otherwise, the whole thing would have started to look like something that survived the journey through a black hole's hurricanes of gravitational forces.

The city's huge furniture factory was constantly pumping out steam and smoke, inhaling and exhaling clouds of workers in three shifts. I could never understand as a kid how all that industrial might could produce things, which were so flimsy, so dysfunctional, and so sensitive to every air current in the house. Later I understood that it was one of the many perfect, tangible, and small-scale representations of the entire regime…

Castles and mansions, sprinkled by a magic hand among the valleys and mountains of Transylvania, have been inspiring dark stories and fairy tales for centuries - but they have also witnessed the house-devouring monster that replaced the dazzling colours of the past with a monotonous nothingness. That urban monster changed its appearance around those castles, as if the magic of those mountains and all-knowing forests had some influence on it.

Countless castles that had not been transformed into hunting lodges for Ceausescu's entourage were mostly looted at the arrival of Communism. We will never know the approximate list of furniture and artworks that had disappeared.

These hills, valleys, and omnipotent-looking, but so helpless, mountains had inspired many tales. During the communist regime more tangible and, unfortunately, more realistic stories circulated about criminally stupid party activists who melted down gold artefacts, destroyed paintings, and burned furniture. There was nothing special about such stories; such things happened everywhere on the advent of communism. These stories were melting fiction and non-fiction together exactly as those vandal bonfires of the communists had done with jewellery...

I could see the remains of these places during the walks and fishing trips of my childhood. By then, the magnificent castles along the river Maros had already been reduced to quietly crumbling carcasses.

Some had a slightly better fate, like the castle at Gernyeszeg (or Gornesti) that was turned into an orphanage after the looting. Other such buildings had been turned into agricultural storage places. Even the priceless mosaics had been destroyed by the pitchforks, and it was impossible to tell the line between intentional vandalism and ignorant savagery.

It is deeply and painfully ironic that those buildings, after they had survived the thunderous and blustery Transylvanian centuries, succumbed to the communists' pitchforks...

Under an ingenious scheme that filled his Swiss bank accounts, Ceausescu was selling the German ethnic minority to West Germany for a few thousand Deutschmarks per head, a sum paid by the West German government – so he let the German minority emigrate.

While this was good news for those who decided to leave the country, it also meant that many villages and small towns have become unpopulated. They had turned into ghost villages; some are there for all to see to this day. Most of them, after their lifeblood had dripped away toward distant lands, were ultimately removed from sight: they were bulldozed to the ground; houses, churches and graveyard were erased for good. It was a different, but genetically related monster to the one, which was erasing historic houses in our cities…

Instead of Stalin's rapid extermination of the villages that refused to join his communist co-operative, our Leader unleashed a slower death that left behind the desiccated bones of local communities and cultures...

V. HEAT

The same irrational energy saving measures that used to plunge us into darkness on a regular basis also included fuel rationing for cars and restrictions on central heating.

Toward the end of the 1970s, the regime introduced a surreal scheme: on even days, the cars with plates ending in an even number were allowed to be on the roads, while on odd days the drivers of cars with odd numbers could celebrate... This scheme applied to all civilian vehicles, and it was intended to reduce the public's fuel consumption.

Ceausescu had set out to pay off all the national debt; fuel economy became just one of the many schemes that were supposed to fill everyone with a deep sense of patriotic duty. It certainly made filling the fuel tanks much more difficult...

The rationing of central heating was also quite... patriotic. Luckily, we lived in an old house; deep brown terracotta stoves heated it, their hot hearts used to pulsate with the flames of natural gas. For me, these stoves were the symbols of priceless warmth – especially as these made us independent of the communal heating systems, which were supposed to keep blocks flats warm.

One must note though, that under the Transylvanian plateau there was, and still is, a huge reserve of natural gas, so this was never in short supply. However, energy saving measures meant that the distribution company began to mix the gas with air in such proportions that it could not lead to explosions, only to colder stoves... and, of course, huge gas bills. We chose to have some decent temperatures in the house, so we were paying enormous gas bills.

The white buildings of the communal heating centres speckled the crowded, but desolate-looking, leaden deserts filled with blocks of flats. For a few hours per day, those centres pumped lukewarm water through tedious networks of dreadfully insulated pipes into the rusty radiators in the apartments.

Dark jokes used to circulate about those heating systems. The hottest things in those apartments were the inhabitants' bodies, some said. By eating chalk or catching flu, one could have dramatically increased the heating efficiency in one's flat, others said.

Often, it was more pleasant to have a vigorous walk outside in the winter cold than to sit around in the cold flats. No migratory being had ever walked from somewhere cold to somewhere much colder in order to warm up... except the millions of supposedly patriotic characters of this communist tragicomedy.

Engineers who thought up schemes for improving various heating systems used to receive praise and prizes for their "heroic innovations".

Some of these "heroes" made use of the warm water from the cooling units of the nearby chemical plant. They pumped the water through several miles of pipework, built at some cost; those pipes had quite useless thermal insulation. When the water eventually reached and gurgled through the radiators of the blocks of flats, it was only able to warm the metal surfaces very gently. Considering the very mild temperatures that these radiators reached, the joke about human bodies being better at warming the flats actually became a physical fact.

Electrical heaters used to help a little bit, but, of course, those were affected by power cuts. In addition, those heaters easily brought families above their monthly electricity consumption quota - and then they experienced a more permanent power cut...

In those concrete deserts, thermal erosion was something more peculiar than the thermal erosion in other, natural, deserts. There were temperature swings, but not between very hot and very cold – only between moderately warm and very cold. This cold, combined with regular darkness, was eroding the human spirit, too.

Whenever spring came to these crowded geometric wastelands, administrators of the heating (or rather, almost-warming) centres used to realise that the fuel quotas for the respective fiscal year had to be used up; otherwise, they would have had their quotas cut in the following year. It remains a mystery why they used to worry about the quotas; after all, they were not renowned for having sleepless nights about proper heating. Still, the net result of their odd and annually recurring angst was that, irrespective of the weather, they began to burn the leftover fuel. Outside one had maybe 24 degrees centigrade brought by a warm March. Inside, one had insanely hot temperatures, even with all the windows open. Again, many were better off outside the flats.

For workers, the eight daily hours spent with the building of the communist future did not get any warmer either during winter. However, in theory, they were being heated from within by the revolutionary zeal... Perhaps something was wrong with my Dad in that particular department, or the theory was not correct... He used to leave our warm house at dawn, so that he could catch an unheated bus that used to glide over freaky, frozen roads. It used to roll slowly uphill to the factory, somehow managing to defy the laws of friction and gravity.

My Dad had spent his working years as a designer of high-pressure plastic injection moulds for car parts and home appliances. He used to calculate and draw them by hand, on A0 sheets of paper. During each winter, he had to wear double gloves - but even so, his hands were so cold that very often he could not properly grab the pencils... His eyes used to water all the time due to the cold air in the office; an icy breeze used to come into the offices due to the badly insulated metal frames of the huge windows.

He rarely talked about it, he just shrugged shoulders whenever I asked how was it possible to work and think in those conditions. He somehow managed not to make serious mistakes in his designs. Miscalculations could have triggered a Kafkaesque investigation into deliberate sabotage. One was guilty until one proved one's own innocence... and anything the local Party activist said was an absolute, it was not open to debate.

A few close encounters with the suited dragons of the regime did occur, but to my father's luck (and ours), the scary problems that were escalated to higher Party officials turned out to be manufacturing, and not design, faults.

At least our classrooms were heated to a temperature that allowed some thinking to take place, and we were able to write without having to wear gloves.

Cinemas, theatres and concert halls were not exempt either from the experiments conducted on our tolerance levels. We used to take with us to the cinema a thermos with hot tea, and hoped that the crowd squeezed into the cinema would warm things up eventually.

Small cinemas were always the worst. The fire exit doors had no insulation to speak of. While we were trying to concentrate on the movie, we had to block out mentally the arctic breezes that used to wander around under our seats. No matter how many and what kinds of socks I wore in my boots, sitting for two hours in these cinemas made catching a cold an inevitability.

At least libraries were allowed to preserve their book collection in some more normal temperatures. Of course, there had to be exceptions. The *Teleki* library, with its rare book collection that belonged to the Hungarian count of same name, was not properly heated.

After all, merely some priceless Hungarian books and manuscripts were slowly disintegrating there, due to wildly fluctuating temperatures and humidity. If those winters had happened many more times, if those heating arrangements had remained as they were, probably most of those manuscripts would have turned into homogeneous cellulose...

In a world where human losses did not matter, the cultural losses, especially those of another culture, were a truly insignificant affair.

VI. PRAISE

Our everyday routines were quite often abruptly interrupted by hours, and sometimes days, of coerced applauding. Festive days in the calendar used to bring these fits of artificial cheers and applauses in a more predictable manner.

The most important date was 23 August, the day of the alleged victory of the Communist Party-led forces against the German occupation, toward the end of the Second World War. There were various made-up dates of our Leader's biography, and other made-up dates of various communist victories over various things... Frankly, one can no longer remember all that random nonsense.

However, less predictable things parachuted into our daily routine - whenever the closest Carpathian equivalent of God decided to visit our city.

The mechanics of these so-called working visits were always rather simple: he came, he waived from his enormous car, we waived back, cheered or at least applauded, he whooshed past us, and we went home... Sometimes we had to wait, depending on the season, in minus 20 degrees centigrade or plus 35 degrees for his departure, too, and repeat the theatrics. On those occasions, the cheers that accompanied his exit were usually more energetic and sincere...

Such sudden visits were always more entertaining than the major "historic" events that we had to celebrate with monotonous recurrence. To this day, I cannot figure out whether by the late 70s he was in such a mental state that he genuinely believed his own fictions, or the celebrations were arranged just to keep up appearances… Maybe it was both.

His visits' simple mechanics were always overshadowed by the whole show. The myriad flags and people were merely the standard ingredients in the special paint that such regimes used in the grand tableaus of homage to our Leader. However, the way in which they used to alter reality was more remarkable.

The shop windows, always barren, depressing, and sometimes decorated with some silly bits of plastic, used to be transformed before his arrival into framed, glass-covered Romanian orthodox icons of abundance. The shops, of course, were closed… Fruits, tropical fruits! Chocolate! Fresh bread! Imported goods! Objects that we used to amaze us were brought from some magic warehouse of the Party.

These were just fleeting hallucinations, strange glimpses into a normality that had existed before the era of food rationing… but these metamorphoses of the shop windows were nothing compared to other more grandiose illustrations of faked plenitude.

On very hot summer days, soldiers used to spray the trees' foliage with green paint before the grand visits. The leaves reliably died later, but at least they looked beautifully fresh and green when the Leader whooshed past them. Even the leaves scorched by the July heat had the duty to look fresh and full of energy.

On one occasion, I could not figure out the source of a mighty stench, which was coming from the other side of the river. There was a village on that side, and agricultural land – but the stench was definitely not that of fertilisers. Eventually we figured out that the stench was coming from rotting cabbages that soldiers and workers had placed in perfect rows on those fields. That literally stinking comedy was staged because the gathering of the crop had already happened before the great Leader's visit.

The logistics of the whole affair had been a blooming (well, actually rotting) nightmare... so the removal of the cabbages after the visit was not on the agenda. Thus nature and, above all, entropy took their course; for the following few weeks, the stench in a radius of many miles was unbearable. The important thing was that a temporary, and thoroughly artificial, reality worked perfectly during the visit.

However, the things that always did disappear promptly after such visits were the fleeting symbols of abundance in the shop windows. The items, which used to appear so magically, used to disappear equally swiftly to the warehouses and special shops that served the Party elite. The major calendar dates' celebrations had less absurd comedy, but it used to take us many days of compulsory rehearsals until everyone got the moves and marches right – then we could create the mandatory visual perfection.

Somehow, all the major historic events pulled off by the communist heroes had fallen on sizzling summer or bitter cold winter days... I never understood as a kid why those heroes could not have done something awesome and utterly world altering during some cosy and bearable season. Maybe the rains of those months had been diluting their world-changing zeal into emotions that were more limited to just sitting at home and planning grand revolutions for very hot or very cold months.

During our forced exhibitions of fake gratitude and joy, certain chapters of physics and anatomy used to be ignored by the organisers... We were not allowed to leave and thus break the geometric patterns constructed in His honour, while other parts of the big picture were rehearsed and tweaked. As a nine-year-old boy, who had to stand still on a cold November morning for several hours, I realised that no patriotic or other emotion could warm one up at such rehearsals. The white nylon pioneer shirts worn by us probably looked great against the green backdrop of a hill or in the stadium where we used to rehearse. We became overheated or frozen pixels in huge faked pictures of joy and gratitude.

My parents had enough of the fact that every such pixelisation of my body was promptly followed by periods of illness. These kept me in bed with fever and bronchitis that used to decide to steer towards random asthma attacks whenever it felt like. It used to make me sound like some bionic version of a smaller bagpipe; sometimes it escalated to levels that needed cortisone injections. We had to find a doctor who was brave enough to sign medical papers that stated, "to whom it may concern", that I was exempt from the process of being turned into a pixel in some glorious picture.

Therefore, I could stay in school or at home during the rehearsals and the celebrations. Still, we often received evening visits from the head teacher or some other servile school staff; they wished to talk to my parents and check my state. I remember even some lovely schoolmates, who, maybe due to a lack of understanding about the world they lived in (or, actually, a premature understanding of how they could score points in it), could state things like "well, he was perfectly fine the day before"... Then it used to take my parents hours and hours to carefully explain that yes, this was a chronic condition triggered by a whole list of things, including the process of using my body as a tiny dot in a huge picture...

Sometimes, our grudging and minimum level of we-are-here-we-have-to-be-here-but-don't-expect-euphoria cheering was not sufficient. There used to be comments from teachers, who used to do the rallies out of genuine conviction or opportunism - comments on how hard we should have applauded, waved, or shouted.

However, technology was there to help – and not just in the TV studios that used to add recorded tsunamis of applause and cheering. Technology was helping on the streets, too - among the trees, there were speakers blasting the same sound waves that used to turn our increasingly lethargic acting into real *tours de force*.

VII. METAL

The thick, grey brushstrokes that the regime used to paint over the map of Romania, as it built new cities or transformed old ones, were outperformed by the megalomaniacal projects that created monolithic symbols of the regime's industrial might.

Ceausescu wanted to turn a predominantly agricultural country rapidly into an industrial power. It was hardly an original or novel idea in the select club of communist dictators. After all, what other greater sign of power could be displayed in front of a sceptical world, than dark and mighty giants producing vast amounts of...stuff. Those industrial giants stretched their muscles over many square miles, and their breath over many layers of the atmosphere.

Thus, a truly immense metallurgical plant in *Galati* was producing huge amounts of cheap and bad quality steel. Bad quality aluminium was produced in *Slatina*, via ancient and tragicomically energy-inefficient methods. A huge chemical plant at the edge of my hometown was producing rudimentary fertilisers... The list was almost endless.

In my hometown, we had our own extra-special summer storm alert system. The chemical plant had been built just outside the city, but then the city grew – and it tiptoed closer and closer to the stinky monster that was huffing and puffing its bad breath. A high school classmate of mine was living close to it, in a newly built grey box, in a newly established concrete desert. He used to laugh at the fact that any washing that his mother hung out to dry acquired a subtle yellow tint. I do not know what his lungs looked like, but I know from my own experience that the number of asthma cases skyrocketed after the plant had been built. This was a correlation that the doctors did not really dare to report.

So why was it such a good storm alert system? Well, whenever we went fishing on the riverside, at the very other end of the city, we could see the yellow smoke rising above the chemical plant. We always packed up and ran home, whenever that smoke began to float horizontally – it was a sure sign of a storm coming, as warm layers of air were pushed down by the approaching weather front.

That industrial monster also used to exhale ammonia, so autumns were characterised by a razor sharp aroma that drifted across the city. For me, walks during the hours of the ammonia attacks usually ended up with asthma attacks triggered by the inhalation of what felt like clouds of tiny razor blades. The smell of ammonia in the morning did indeed "smell like victory", but it was the dubious victory of the communist industrial revolution over sanity...

The main train line that crosses the city had been built next to that chemical plant, so whenever I travelled on a late night train I knew even with my eyes closed when I reached or exited my hometown – as the changes in the concentration of industrial monster's stench were as precise as GPS.

There were also high-tech factories that produced electronic calculators, even computers the size of industrial washing machines, home appliances, cars - and the regime was exporting them. It was a clear sign of their quality that the attempts to export them, even to other communist countries, often failed.

Somehow, the regime's pride in the country's industrial might did not conflict with the leader's idea of imitating Western technology. Poorly imitating, one might add.

For example, in the case of a factory that made all sorts of electrical gizmos and where my Dad worked, the Party used to allow a few chosen people to travel to some close-by capitalist countries. They used to bring back hair driers, heaters, car radios, portable Hi-Fi systems; these were then disassembled and reverse-engineered. A major task was to figure out some cheap way of imitating them.

For my Dad, the not amusing aspect of this otherwise tragicomic replication of Western products was the task of designing the high-pressure plastic injection moulds; whatever was ejected from those had to successfully imitate the original parts. The capitalist engineers had designed the original products, later copied by the communist revolutionaries, with state-of-the-art tools that included computer models. In comparison, my father had to approximate the shape of the parts, tediously plot it on paper with geometric approximations - and then design the injection moulds for them. I remember how he used to come home, still cursing the complicated curves and surfaces of the objects that he had to analyse and replicate...

However, the geometry of those plastic objects was nothing compared to the nightmare of the actual plastic materials... The revolutionary managers in those factories often forgot that, despite our mighty chemical industry led by the allegedly renowned scientist Elena Ceausescu (the dictator's wife who could barely read), we simply did not possess the advanced plastics that allowed one to produce those objects.

Thus, the mishaps in the prototyping departments were tragicomic. It was very difficult and quite dangerous to explain to the Party officials the fact that utterly crappy plastics were not state-of-the-art polymers, therefore the often-undesirable results were not caused by sabotage.

While all this was going on, we were being told in schools, and in the media, that eighty per cent of all goods produced by our industry had the same quality as those made by the West... and that the other twenty percent was of *better* quality.

Even for a kid, the double contradiction was simply

hilarious. On one hand, everything from toys to household objects used to fall apart in our hands – often literally. Unless of course, they were imported from the Soviet Union - those toys were over-engineered, virtually indestructible wonders that used to last forever. On the other hand, the regime was always looking down on the capitalist countries and their industry - but it was desperately copying their products, and constantly setting absurd targets to match their quality...

A further absurdity was that despite all of the astounding crap produced by these mega-factories, industry secrets were managed with great deal of care. My father had to go through tedious processes to take home some hand-drawn designs from the archives. My precocious sarcasm was flexing its adolescent muscles back then; I voiced my opinion that those drawings were ultra-secret in order to avoid killing foreign spies – because latter would have laughed themselves to death if they ever saw the schematics.

The Genius of the Carpathian Mountains, to quote one of the official terms for our leader, used to visit the factories quite regularly; he was always telling workers and managers what to do, how to improve and what to strive for. He was an expert in everything from mechanical engineering to mixing of concrete to microelectronics... Very few such people had ever walked the face of the Earth since Leonardo da Vinci...

Therefore, clearly, our Leader really was a rare breed. His wife, too, Elena, the allegedly internationally renowned scientist that nobody ever heard of in academic circles, was a powerhouse of ideas. Glass cabinets in every school and library were full of books allegedly written by her and published in many languages. Those works had received many never-heard-of prizes from mythical foreign institutions.

These two luminaries had thought that they could really change the world. Thank God, some changes were averted in time... For example, in the case of the building of the nuclear power plant at *Cernavoda*. The project was supervised by Canadian experts, and this proved to be a vital detail.

One day, the intellectual giants visited the site. We learnt from *Radio Free Europe* that the reason for the immense delays to the project was caused by the leader's clever advice. The precious Leader had given instructions to alter the design of the reactor building. Apparently, he had instructed the workers to make the, in his mind wastefully thick, concrete walls much thinner.

A few weeks later, the Canadian inspectors landed in Bucharest, and they were taken to what by then had become a giant experiment in interesting aspects of chaos theory... They took one look at it... and promptly got back on the next flight out of Romania. They made it clear, that they will not have anything to do with the project until the whole thing is rebuilt based on the original design. Later we heard in the national media that *they* had deliberately sabotaged us... of course...

Around the same time, I remember that we were quite worried about my first cousin, because his military service posted him close to the capital. It was a tradition during the regime's ethnic homogenisation policy, as it was called, to send Transylvanian ethnic minorities as far as possible from their home environment. As a result, he, too, ended up at the other end of the country. However, location itself was not the reason for our worry – a major construction project was. Latter, in a very wobbly and lethargic fashion, walked off the planning sheets and headed toward physical reality – and the army, as usual, had to give a helping hand with its journey.

My cousin, together with who knows how many soldiers, spent most of his military service driving enormous trucks in the far South of the country. They transported the excavated soil away from the vast building site, where Ceausescu was shaping his grand dream: the Danube-Black Sea canal. Many soldiers died during its construction, as untrained men and teenage boys were handling machinery that they had no real training for.

Thankfully, my cousin returned alive, although he was much skinnier and he had visibly aged. A few years later, Ceausescu could finally celebrate the completion of his much too shallow and largely unusable canal. It, after another few years, became completely unusable due to sedimentation...

Sometimes, we could benefit from some admirable efforts by the communist industry. During high school, the only computers we saw in real life were those shown to us during visits to local so-called computing centres. We used to admire the enormous computers, which looked like the results of the crossbreeding of close-to-extinction dinosaurs and industrial refrigerators... Eventually, thanks to the commendable efforts of some clever people, we had access to personal computers in our labs.

Some of these computers were produced based on local designs, and they were not compatible with anything else under the Sun. Other types of computers were reverse-engineered; these were claimed to be 99% compatible with ZX-Spectrums. I still remember with awe these mechanically flimsy, but utterly clever concoctions, which resulted from the efforts of a few computing enthusiasts. They figured out what the highly integrated chips in the Spectrums were doing, and designed the equivalent digital hardware with many smaller general-purpose digital chips. The resulting machines were much bigger than the original, but they managed to imitate its functionality... and they worked beautifully.

The computing and electronics labs in schools were definitely many years behind what Western kids could play with; still, these were high-tech little islands where the tidal waves of ideological crap could not reach us. The one good thing about the regime's obsession with the creating the New Man, the New Society, was that it channelled considerable resources toward high-tech hobbies. Camps were organised every summer for 'techie' kids. Endless series of competitions and symposia were organised for pupils; they could present there designs and talked about how they had translated those into working gizmos. For me, hobby electronics was definitely a refuge from the tides of Communist propaganda that was raging outside the old walls of my high school.

However, this was a two-way street - we had to play our part in the glorious march of the communist industry. Every school had to have a close relationship with some nearby factory. When I was tiny, we used to go to a local factory that produced canned fruits; we spent there a few weeks during each school trimester, washed and peeled fruits. Later, as our skills and usefulness improved with age, we began to make things. In the last years of secondary school and later in high school, we made door hinges, parts for ladders, and other such nonsense.

During high school, some special agreement between the school's leadership and the person who was teaching some of us hobby electronics allowed us to avoid the so-called practical weeks of the school calendar. Instead of making silly metal parts manually, we could sit in the computing and electronics labs, making fun things that may not have had industrial use – but they sure made us happy.

VIII. SCHOOL

The regime, in its quest for perfect-looking fake images of its present, had become desperate to alter its past. It changed history many times – not via time travel, but via a quite postmodern mix of fiction and non-fiction wrapped in ideology.

"Sands of time" is a clichéd expression, but the regime had indeed been treating us to a continuously shifting sand of regularly revised and re-written history. That history's often-fictional battlefields were covered with many landmines made of dangerous dogmas.

Most of the time, the only new schoolbooks that turned up in the foul-smelling storeroom of my school were the ones of history and literature. Mathematics, physics, chemistry, biology always filled the pages of old books - after all, these subjects were immune to shifting ideological viewpoints.

Literature books were full of re-interpreted writers, who had created works that caught the censors' attention. Some authors had written with intentionally hidden meanings, or their works just happened to lead to mental associations that people should not have had. Sometimes the works themselves were fine, but their authors had ended up in conflict with the regime. Such writers, together with their works, used to vanish. Their existence used to be erased; schoolbooks were revised and reprinted during the few hot months of summer.

History needed many reprints; after all, it was full of battles between ideas, principles, and facts; many events were destined for reinterpretation and, in our case, heavy censoring.

In many ways, literature and history were combined when the regime's best censors-cum-inventors came up with the rewrites. The regime was incapable of altering its future (as it became apparent on 22 December 1989), but it managed to construct a painstakingly detailed fake tableau of its past.

In fourth grade, we were taught the country's history in one way. That same history was later repeated to us in more detail during eighth grade - but many things changed on the pages of the revised schoolbooks. During high school, yet another inventive metamorphosis of history happened. Very sensitive chapters, like those related about Transylvania, Hungary, WW2 and the role of the Party, were rewritten several times.

If one had good marks, then one had the dubious honour of being made into "commander" of the communist youth... This had meant not only that one had to be present in that capacity at all the mass rallies, but also one was sent to various communist youth conferences and meetings. Presence was obligatory, although one did not do much at either type of events...

Occasionally, one had to write some carefully vetted nonsense about the pupils' achievements, with the obligatory thanks to the Party, and read the nonsense at these meetings. I admit, I did not have the courage to refuse, and nobody else did... I could easily slap myself nowadays, whenever I think back to those years and those speeches, as it is unclear what consequences a refusal would have had. Probably nothing severe, but who knows... Still, we were only kids and we used to join the theatrics to some extent; it was the least risky thing to do.

Amongst all this fluidity, the school days' routine used to be rock solid. Those were the days of wonderful travels of the mind; our vehicles were just some chalk on some antediluvian blackboard, some voices, some hand gestures – and, sometimes, bits of utterly fascinating equipment in a physics or a chemistry lab.

It may sound odd, but I am extremely grateful for the desperate shortcomings of those mini-worlds that existed behind the bland concrete walls of our school.

In the absence of well-equipped classrooms and labs, and in the presence of a firm ideology that wanted to suppress too far-reaching thoughts, we learnt to imagine things. We used to visualise ancient battles, all the details of the dust clouds stirred up by heels of human, semi-human, or godly creatures...

My favourite music teacher used to bring us old records that she played on an ancient turntable, thus she could demonstrate rather abstract musical theories in action. I still vividly recall her games. For example, she played selected pieces from Mussorgsky's *Pictures at an Exhibition*, and we had to guess which painting was depicted by which musical piece whose sounds used to tiptoe out of the battered wooden box of the mono speaker.

She also used to send us to educational concerts. Those were magical... We could watch grownups play with invisible machinery in a huge reverberating engine room that the city's concert hall temporarily became for us.

The city's much-respected Philharmonic on those Sunday mornings used to deconstruct light Mozart or Haydn pieces, showing us the musical components that hovered in the air... First, they made us hear the notes played by the violins only, then the violas, then something else and something else and then... there was magic!

They assembled for us the sometimes strangely shaped sonic parts, with the help of magical tools at their disposal, using invisible blueprints made in the air by the tip of the conductor's baton... and *voilà*!... a familiar piece... The huge musical engine was assembled from its myriad parts, and it was purring nicely, smoothly, obediently; the well-lubricated notes were gliding over the soft rhythms, playfully complex and invisible cogs were held together by the intricate laws we learnt about during music lessons.

Abstract concepts, counterpoints, harmonies, chord resolutions - all became tangible in that engine room, all had shapes, tastes, and colours...

The conductor had spent many hours with thinking up new and playful ways to make us feel the taste of a chord, the colour of a counterpoint. He had thought of matching the musical program to the seasons, so he brought the heat of the sunshine, the odours of the spring rain, the crisp sounds of the snow into the concert hall.

The school buildings are worth remembering, but only my high school triggers special memories. My primary and secondary school, which used to absorb and then secrete masses of kids every day, was just a bland concrete block with square windows and dreary repetitions of rectangular patterns. Its appearance was marginally enhanced by some yellow paint that alternated with the dominant whitish-grey architectural lethargy.

The courtyard behind it was a reasonably large one - after all, it had to accommodate the hundreds of tiny bodies that used to boil or shiver there, depending on the weather, while some communist blah blah was being broadcasted via a rudimentary speaker system.

The classrooms, filled with old wood benches, were so criminally non-ergonomic that they would have made osteopaths very rich in a market economy. Those rooms were also an exercise in communist minimalism: they only contained *the* portrait, a blackboard, and benches. To save electricity, every second light bulb or neon tube was removed in the late '70s...

Some teachers, who had a laboratory at their command, managed to make the lessons infinitely more enjoyable and intriguing. I loved the biology and chemistry lessons, oh, and the physics lab! It was pure pleasure for the eyes and for curious minds... Its walls were covered with wood and glass cabinets, shelves upon shelves filled with strange metal, crystal and plastic objects waiting for somebody to lift them onto a desk, to give them a nudge, to give them life... so that they could make intricate laws of the Universe visible and tangible for us.

As I was passionate about maths and physics, it was fairly obvious to me and my parents that I should attempt to get into the strongest high school in Transylvania. The *Farkas Bolyai* high school had almost 500 years of history; the father of *János Bolyai*, the inventor of non-Euclidian geometry, had taught mathematics there in the 19th century.

The entrance exams to this school were tough, because for each available place there were at least 4-6 pupils competing... I managed to get in, so, suddenly, that enormous building on the top of a hill, close to my home, became my everyday reality. This put an end to my wondering about what went on inside that enigmatic, mythical edifice, behind its enormous gates and two feet thick walls...

It had vast corridors with tall ceilings and rich decorations, imposing staircases and spacious classrooms, laboratories filled with gadgets. Vast acoustic spaces were bouncing our voices between the mighty walls of the gymnasium, old portraits of teachers and pupils from vintage years filled the walls of the corridors... It was a completely different world, compared to my old school that I had left behind in 1986.

My daily walks to and from the high school's most recent wing, built in glorious eclectic style, were taking me under the arches created by rows of friendly trees, past the medieval city walls and the gothic church therein... No more walks among depressing blocks of flats...

I could sit inside grandiose architecture dreamt up by the genius that was *György Bernády*, who had created the famous look of the city centre at the beginning of the 20th century. Instead of grey block flats, there is a park in front of the school, surrounded by other historical buildings. Among those stands the vast library of count Teleki, with myriad books that he had collected from all over the world. It is a lovely pastel-coloured building, and it hosts first editions of Kepler's Celestial Mechanics, works by Galilei, ancient manuscripts in Hungarian, calendars and maps from the Far East...

It was a vastly different world, with teachers who made sure that we could graduate with excellent chances of being admitted to the best Universities in the country.

Of course, there were aberrations, too. Some teachers, whom we labelled "unsafe", used to make us stand up and sing the national anthem. They had been brainwashed or they were trying to score points with the regime's local activists. We could never tell, so judgments materialised quickly in our teenage minds... Others, who had taught philosophy or other "dangerous" humanist subjects that could have made pupils think outside the box, were turned into teachers of subjects like communist political economics.

Foreign languages, too were taught, usually Russian and something else... The former was taught by a national treasure, who had dedicated his life to this language imposed by the regime. He had written the reference schoolbook that was available in both Romanian and Hungarian languages in the country's high schools. He was renowned for his terrifying rigour - he used to fail most pupils every trimester. Well, we ended up hating the subject he had been teaching.

We never had a problem with Russian *per se*. Its phonemes, and its soft, bubbly constructs were beautiful when they carried the poetry of Esenin on their sound waves – but it was the mother tongue of the monster, which had swallowed Eastern Europe.

Due to the school's history, many Hungarian ethnic parents were hoping to have their kids study there. There was also quite some camaraderie between the Hungarian pupils and teachers; hence, we used to feel relatively safe whenever we talked about things that we would not have voiced on the streets.

Therefore, this quasi-fortress of ethnic and ideological resistance had attracted the special attention of the regime. Contributing to the tension, there used to be quite a competition between the nearby *Alexandru Papiu-Ilarian* high school, the similar citadel of regional Romanian education, and us. Local officers of the Securitate and Party elite each year were trying (and, of course, always managing) to send their kids to study there.

Therefore, any student competition or symposium meant that the two strongest high schools in the region, certainly the most talked-about ones, made their delegates feel the extra tension caused by ideological and ethnic undertones. Hungarian kids just had to be inferior in the regime's mind... but fortunately, Bolyai often came out on top, to the immense pride of our teachers. One almost feels guilty when one reminisces over those things; why on Earth were we made to feel that we had to prove something just because of our different ethnicity?

Honest to God, whom I had been having a very difficult relationship with during those years, I just wanted to be *myself*. I did not want to be characterised purely by my ethnic origin in many everyday situations that had been distorted by the Ceausescu regime's ideology.

I could not have predicted that the enormous fortress-like building of my high school would later become a shelter during the ethnic pogrom, which was unleashed in my hometown just three months after the 1989 Revolution. Once again, the Bolyai high school became a symbol of the struggle for ethnic minority rights...

IX. FOOD

During the years of food rationing, eating was often a mystery and an adventure combined. There were countless jokes about what one could find in bread, minced meat, or in the occasionally available salami. Bits of string, plastic or bone fragments were easy to spot, but some more subtle ingredients were present, too.

Sausages were practically vegetarian sausages, considering the amount of soy and other "secret ingredients" that they contained.

An entire science, and an industry, of fake ingredients had developed. Even the flour used in bread was replaced with odd mixtures of who knows what. Bread used to make crunchy noises between my teeth; it made me think that I was perhaps eating a vintage blend of finest sand and sawdust, combined with some flour.

Chocolate did not contain much real cocoa or cocoa butter; it was mostly made from brownish chicory. Hence, so-called chocolate was a powdery, sawdust-like, and rather bitter substance. Real coffee was just a trace element in the boxes of chicory sold as coffee – chicory had become the magical multi-purpose ingredient...

I felt a huge admiration and respect for the confectioners

and bakers of those times. They had invented whole volumes of original recipes, which used ingenious replacements for unavailable key ingredients. They used to create superb éclairs from God knows what; however, in contrast with the earlier mentioned biochemical assaults on our digestive tracks, these creations' taste was *heavenly*. The amaretto base of chocolate cakes was imitated with a mysterious blend of very basic ingredients, with some minced biscuit and flavouring. The various liqueur flavours were imitated via synthetic "essences"; these came in various colours and tastes located at the ultra-heavenly end of the spectrum.

Ice cream was made from milk substitutes and some weird sugary concentrate; lemon used to come from citric acid solution that was coloured with something. Nobody really knew what was going on in the small temples of sweet, edible poetry.

We always used to consume the results of these creative struggles after our visits to the canine exhibitions. We used to pamper all sorts of dangerously cute dogs that were exhibited among the medieval walls of the city, and then we visited the nearby *Intim* cafeteria. We used to sit there for an hour or so and slowly consumed the sinful poems that the magicians, or deities, or some combination of both had concocted for us. The illusion was perfect.

Our festive meals used to be... relatively festive. For Christmas and New Year's Eve, we used to accumulate some meat and some dubious frankfurters in the freezer from a few months' rations. Some illegal house wine, made in our cellar by my Dad and my godfather, used to serve as an extra touch...

Foreign visitors, like my uncle from West Germany and other relatives from Hungary, had to phone in advance with their precise plans - hopefully not weeks, but months in advance. Of course, this was not always possible. The reason for this extended warning period was that we had to try to accumulate some meat in the freezer from our monthly rations, so that we could cook for them something decent.

Going out to restaurants was not really an option. After all, very few restaurants existed in the whole city; most of them were serving truly diabolical food with ludicrous price tags, while others were reserved for the Party elite...

Therefore, hospitality used to include some theatre, with many stage props of normality. This was not meant to construct a fake image for our guests, as they were well aware of the real situation; instead, the theatre was there to avoid making them feel awkward. Otherwise, they would have seen constant reminders of the fact that they were consuming several months' worth of meat rations during their stay...

Schools used to help the food industry and agricultural exports with the manual gathering of apples, cherries, carrots, grapes. We were taken to the farms by almost-wrecked buses; we used to imagine that only a pair of wheels would remain, once the buses scattered all of their mechanical components, and us, on those roads.

We were not self-consciously rebelling against the regime at the age of eight or nine. Still, we used to notice some signals from certain teachers, who were enforcing way too keenly every stupid rule of the regime. Hence, our "rebellion" consisted of just scoring some points against these teachers...

One of our methods was the use selective hearing, whenever they were telling us that each apple must be picked carefully from the tree. Instead, we used to shake the branches as hard as we could, then we quickly gathered the fallen apples. We used to enjoy this very much, since we knew that those battered apples, which were destined for export, would turn into horrid-looking brownish objects a few days later. We were not allowed to take any apples home – and this turned us into even more hardened little rebels.

Like in the case of the shop windows that used to be temporarily filled with goodies during the Leader's visits, it was unclear to us where exactly all those grapes and apples used to end up. Clearly, they were not usually sent to our shops...

When very occasionally they did turn up in shops, the news of the miracles used to spread rapidly. An old woman, who lived two houses away from us, used to run back from the city centre on her tiny legs and told everybody that apples had arrived. We then used to initiate one of our family-sized commando missions to the particular shop; after some queuing, we got home with a few kilos of fruits.

We were 20th century Eastern European versions of the ancient hunter-gatherer people.

Whenever potatoes arrived, we used to buy enough to last us through the winter. As we did not have a car, a few roundtrips between the shop and our home used to solve the problem. My mother used to stay behind at the shop and guarded the 80-100 kilos of potatoes we had bought during a successful commando deployment. We used to put the whole lot into our cellar, and, for a few winter months, we had versatile potatoes for cooking all sorts of things.

Food rationing was really introduced during the '80s - exactly when the great Leader, the Genius of the Carpathian Mountains, decided to pay off all of the country's debts.

The best and easiest way of doing this was to export everything he could possibly export. As the products of his industrial giants were not quite up to the standards of the West, he began to export food and timber. This was meant to turn us into a truly sovereign nation, one that was independent of the imperialist world.

The hunt for food and our food rationing coupons made us, kids, feel that we were really contributing to the running of the family. On certain days, when the meat, sugar, or whatever was due to arrive in the shops, people used to queue early in the morning, because latecomers missing out on the limited stocks had to wait until a next, usually uncertain, delivery that came some days later.

Hence, my pensioner grandmother used to start the queuing. I used to go home from school, and if my granny was not at home, I went to the usual shop to relieve her. Then, my mother or father got home from work, and joined the queue; hence, I could go home. After all this fun, eventually my parents got home with the goods: some meat, some sugar or whatever.

The queues often had special guest appearances from informers or agents of the secret police, the *Securitate*; they used to try to provoke people via angry rants about our Leader. Reacting to those rants was very risky; not only reports were then written, but also in serious cases, personalised treatment could occur. After such minor offences, which were labelled "subversive activities", the Securitate used to present the offender with a choice: suffer dire consequences, or become an informer. It was the easiest form of recruitment...

Thinking back now, the filing of all these reports in some Securitate archive would have been quite an idiotic method. However, such methods of "recruiting" informers, together with the spreading of news about occasional example-setting punishments, sustained and amplified the psychological terror.

X. SOUL

The rationing of food for the body used to go hand in hand with the rationing of food for the soul. Soul was not highly rated by the regime; it was just pointless ballast in the dialectic materialist society they were trying to build. Actually, soul was even dangerous...

However, despite the firm and central idea of a society made of *robotniks*, reality was very different. The Romanian orthodox church was not only flourishing, it was actually enjoying countless privileges because it was playing a very vital political role during the regime; it was a crucial and superbly effective component of the propaganda machine. The depth of the collaboration between the regime and that church only became known 18 years after the Revolution, when the relevant files of the Securitate have finally seen the light of day.

The Greco-Catholic church had been suffocated, suppressed, its estates were taken over by the Orthodox Church, and the problems continue to this day. Still, the most threatening religious institutions for the regime had been the Roman Catholic Church and the various protestant Churches. Their congregations consisted of the large Hungarian and not so large German ethnic minorities – basically, people who understood the language of foreign media.

Many churches had vibrant choirs and they were recruiting kids from an early age. Many brave priests held beautiful, and often dangerously subversive, sermons... There is a strong resonance with Salman Rushdie's *The Enchantress of* Florence, in which an Emperor builds a place with the sole intent of creating a space of openness, free thought, and debate. For us, the churches were such places - whether we were practicing our religion or not. Of course, some priests may well have been informers... but at least the illusion of safety, and our ability to debate and voice dangerous thoughts, was enticing and addictive.

These churches were indeed a threat to the regime. After all, a Hungarian Reformed priest, Laszlo Tokes, ignited the 1989 revolution... However, in the everyday life, the regime could not do much to suppress the Hungarian Churches. It took their colleges away (like the former Reformed high school I frequented), and did the same to as many other church-owned estates as it could. The churches themselves remained operational, and they became base camps for the quiet resistance of the not yet atrophied soul. Some churches and chapels in small villages, which had turned into ghost villages once their inhabitants had left, were destroyed – bulldozed, in true Stalinist tradition.

Nobody in our family was really practicing religion, and my parents had felt a certain level of repulsion toward religious institutions. Still, I occasionally attended services in the white gothic church built in 1490 that later had gone through the Reformation. This is where I got hooked on choral music, on organ recitals, while I was sitting on its cold benches. I was, and I remain, completely infatuated with music; I have never had a singing voice, thus the local choir was not something I had contemplated being active in... Therefore, I remained just a fervent "consumer" of music.

I cannot recall how medieval and baroque music became my main passion. It happened early, before I could have any understanding of their structures and their complex inner laws. The music just crept up on me via choral works at first, then via light pieces that used to tiptoe gently around me in the white spaces of that Reformed church. This later made me discover the city's concert hall, where I began to experience magic on a much larger scale...

For me, it is still very difficult to understand the unnatural elitist resonances that are associated nowadays with classical music. It, quite simply, was the *only* (mostly) freely available music that we had access to; it was virtually uncensored, performed all the time, released on vinyls, taught, sold, and played without much restriction.

Still, some ideology was present; after all, a lot of "decadent" 20th century music was frowned upon, but earlier centuries' music was not problematic at all... For us, kids, it was a beautiful and utterly unrestricted escapism.

Thus, never in my life have I regarded classical music or opera as something "reserved" for people with a certain level of IQ or position in society. It was just deeper music that *did* something more to us inside than some three-minute-long pop spasm.

We, of course, consumed the latter at school dances and discotheques, but they could hardly fill our long evenings. Our attention span had not yet shrunk to twenty seconds, so we often listened with undivided attention to hour-long pieces, without interruption of any kind. It was a musical journey, and it created an appetite for album-long compositions in other genres.

Despite all of the official attempts to restrict the importing of contemporary Western pop & rock albums, we could get them from the so-called copying studios. These would have been chronic insomnia-causing horror visions for any copyright lawyer in the Western world. We used to go to these studios-cum-shops with a few cassettes in our pockets, and ordered from a huge catalogue of recordings; then, a few days later, we walked away with 60 or 90 minutes of music copied onto those cassettes. That is how we got our hands on pop and rock albums for our weekend school bashes or house parties; but, more importantly, that is how many of us got hold of entire catalogues of jazz, progressive rock and electronic/space music.

The owner of the copying shop on the *Kossuth* street, located very close to my home, was extremely passionate about his music; he had immense amounts of LPs and reel-to-reel tapes. His wife used to sit at the tiny counter of the tiny shop, and I could see bits of the larger recording area behind her, with many blinking lights on the tape recorders.

I got hooked on "odd" music at an early age and I was a regular customer at the copying shop. I was ordering a lot of electronic music and progressive rock; the large, bearded shop owner was like a musical wizard for me. After all, he could charm magnetic particles into a secret order, so that they could bring to life glorious, and so hard to find, music in my room.

Usually, the process of discovering such music was tedious, but extremely rewarding. I used to stay up late on Sunday evenings, so that I could listen to *Florian Pittis* on the radio. He was one of the very few people in the country who owned a huge collection of rock and jazz albums. I am not sure, how he acquired it, how he managed to become the only person who was allowed to have a radio show like that.

In his weekly hour-long program, he used to talk about some album, and then played it in its entirety, ending the show just before midnight.

No wonder that many progressive rock and ambient music albums were seriously augmented by one's experience of hearing them on the radio, in the dark, whilst one was floating right on the boundary between reality and dreams... To this day, whenever I can, I listen to such records in the dark – mostly due to those late Sunday evenings of musical wonder.

Whenever I heard something on the radio that I really liked, I used to beg my parents for some pocket money. I used to put together enough to buy a cassette and pay for the copying - then I ran to the bearded wizard and his less magical-looking wife...

If I was lucky, he had the album in his catalogue. There were albums, though that I only acquired many years later...

Some were rare, so I had to hunt for them via friends in other towns until I managed to obtain a third-hand cassette copy of the music, with not exactly awesome sound quality. Quality did not matter so much after such a long quest... It was music that used to hover above a gentle, wavy jungle of hissing and popping, the results of vinyl-to-tape copying followed by many tape-to-tape copies...

"Music - the breathing of statues", as Rilke so wonderfully had put it. Music – so mesmerising, that a kid could spend years trying to get his hands on it. Years! An entire underground network of music fanatics existed back then, and we used to help each other with tapes. The luckier ones possessed LPs that had been produced in much more liberal communist countries like Hungary and Yugoslavia.

One interesting side effect of all this was that we really only ever acquired the music itself. In other words, we were often completely disconnected from the visuals and the paraphernalia that used to accompany the creators of, for example, progressive rock albums. While their showmanship had risen to by now proverbial excesses, we only had their music, without the hype and the decadent imagery. Therefore, I still firmly believe that we had a unique chance to connect with the music, and not be influenced by the persona or media image of a certain artist... This, in today's world, is inconceivable...

Another place of musical treasures was the so-called listening room of the city library's music archive. Latter contained tens of thousands of mostly classical albums. As a magical coincidence, a bearded fan of electronic music and progressive rock ran this department of the library.

I was about eleven years old when I discovered those dusty rooms, which had a dozen or so desks; each desk was equipped with a turntable and a pair of headphones. I used to spend hours and hours there, browsing through the catalogue of small, alphabetically ordered cards, asking the staff to bring the vinyl, and then giving it a spin. By the time I got to high school, the bugs of electronic and prog-rock music had terminally infected me.

The opening of a listening room in an old building, which has been hosting the huge library assembled by the late count Teleki, was pure joy for us. On Sundays, the room was always empty in the morning; so, without disturbing anyone, the administrator could play us one of his favourite tapes or LPs on the huge speakers of the listening room. He used to enchant us, musical pilgrims, with a sound quality that I could only dream about when I listened to my portable cassette player.

Thus, many Sunday mornings became strange, but wonderful musical journeys through space and time... Space, because the music always took me to worlds, which I was inventing in my head as the sounds unfolded around me. Time, because it was a wondrous transition from a walk through the old corridors of the building, up on the loudly creaking wooden stairs, to the futuristic electronic soundscapes that emanated from the speakers.

There, I had the opportunity to listen to some minor, but passionate sonic experiments, too. The administrator took Jean-Michel Jarre's mesmerisingly fluid, otherworldly *Oxygène* LP, patched the turntable to four bulky speakers via a quasi-quadraphonic setup. I could sit in the middle of the room; he walked out, and left me there with sounds that turned my mind and soul inside out in ways I could not imagine before. It was music that sounded as if it had not been played by a person; instead, that music was simply happening, it was floating in the air between the thick, old walls, without human intervention, yet it was deeply human and vibrant.

That listening room was the space where I managed to travel to the Himalayas, helped by Vangelis; to the thinking ocean on the planet Solaris, helped by the Japanese magician of sounds, Isao Tomita... and to countless hypnotic planetary landscapes, helped by Klaus Schulze and Jean-Michel Jarre...

If I think back to the various "tribes" of kids in school and later high school, to the groups of heavy metal, prog-rock, and electronic music fans, it is clear to me now that we were not self-consciously choosing to consume western pop tracks only as party music. I believe that it was something subconscious: music that expressed something and works that had been created based on elaborate concepts were vehicles that could take us away from our often-nasty everyday reality.

We used to discuss without any inhibitions what we had been imagining during our listening to such records. We used to get together, play some record, turn off the lights and switch to some other reality - without any chemical aids. Thus, without any snobbery, and via genuinely drug-free escapism, by our late teens we built up a quite deep knowledge of rock, jazz, classical music, and opera.

Nowadays, while I am clicking through some music mail order website, I still cringe if I think back how I had spent many months, sometimes even years, with the quest for some music that I had heard on radio.

How could some sounds get one on the verge of a sweet obsession? It is probably not an accident that we had chosen music, which was always far removed from the world of everyday trivia. In my case, it was usually space music or progressive rock, both highly addictive in their ability to depict some fascinating and very different world.

I loved to be made to feel tiny by such music; however, that sense of insignificance was not the nasty one, which the regime had wanted to create. It was, well, some kind of cosmic insignificance, which made us, the teenagers-turned-space-romantics, realise that none of the grand propaganda speeches meant anything...

XI. REALM

The first photocopier machines made in the country were based on reverse engineered Rank Xerox machines. The output of these copied copiers resembled psychedelic paintings; the quality was simply dreadful. Still, in order to be able to photocopy something, one had to go through a serious vetting process - after all, photocopiers were a perfect tool, if one wanted to produce subversive propaganda material.

Such paranoia was, of course, omnipresent. The regime tried to frighten people with its made-up or real might; however, like all other totalitarian regimes, it was pathologically afraid of "counter-revolutionaries".

We had to be careful not to walk in large groups, because a dozen people gathering somewhere would have been seen as a demonstration. Even as kids, we were often challenged on the street when we went out with classmates and friends to see a movie. Usually some ordinary-looking character began to orbit around us, wanting to find out what we were talking about. Clearly, such practices were not security measures against some genuine threat to the regime; they were just methods devised to make us feel watched all the time.

Of course, the world beyond the Iron Curtain was out to 'get us' via various means. Somehow the decadent imperialist West had not only managed to produce immense wealth compared to our fictional riches, but also in its spare time it allegedly had been spying on us ordinary people. Of course, they had to - we had just too many genii who were running our country and our industry.

Thus, the regime's paranoia used to manifest itself around us regularly; we were able to almost taste it, smell it... This particular variety of paranoia had the metallic taste of irony, with the mouldy aftertaste of the absurd.

For example, despite the fact that we lived in the era of spy satellites, military buildings and army barracks were taboo for anyone equipped with a camera. This applied even to a thirteen-year-old kid equipped with his first manual camera. I had to be ultra-careful not to take pictures in areas marked by big signs that used to show a crossed-out camera. It was a ludicrous concept: a Western spy coming to a town like mine, and having to take photos of these military barracks, standing across the street...

We also found out, with great hilarity, that one of the major railway junctions near my hometown was not actually shown on any civilian maps. This railway station, called Kocsárd (or Razboieni, in Romanian language), apparently had such strategic importance that it had become a non-existent spot on the map. It was hilarious to imagine that a foreign spy of the 1980s would have had to come to a bookstore in Romania to buy a local map for some awesome imperialist war plan.

Such measures meant to defend the allegedly astounding values of our communist society were just the softer versions of the surreal Romanian military comedy. The country's guardians used to remind themselves to train even us, school kids, for the hands-on defence of the realm.

During high school, both boys and girls used to be taken to the shooting ground near the city. This used to happen on sufficiently autumnal days to make the whole experience a rainy, cold, and overall miserable one.

Still, these were fun days away from school, playing with real guns that dated back to the mid-to-late 1950s; they were surreally rudimentary compared to what the decadent imperialists would have attacked us with...

The proud officers used to show us these antique guns, but usually after at least three hours of us waiting for someone to turn up on the hillside – a perfect illustration of the Romanian army's perfect organisational skills. After the demonstrations of once-upon-a-time effective weapons, we could finally get our hands on them. Each of us was then handed four bullets to practise shooting with the relics.

The targets had been planted at some fifty meters distance by someone who must have been thoroughly soaked in large amounts of vodka, or in something functionally equivalent... The targets were off by as much as thirty degrees angle relative to the direction that I, or any sober person on the planet, would have denoted as "right ahead". Whenever I had to take aim, I first had to count in what position I was lying on the ground... then I had count the targets, too, so that I could find mine.

This Romanian military version of "the target in front of me" used to make me end up with more holes on my target than the number of bullets I was given... Obviously, some of us had not counted correctly the targets and, assuming we actually managed to hit something, we shot others' targets - or we possessed superhuman skills...

The bullet casings had to be given back to the soldiers, and the little metal cylinders were carefully counted. However, those old Soviet guns used to spit the casings in random directions at random distances - thus some casings often ended up, well, missing in action...

We then had to form a line and search the ground until we found the missing casings. After several such search parties, always accompanied by screaming and shouting from some demented officers, we always ended up with boxes of leftover ammunition after the target practice – so we had to use them up.

Because of the absurd logic of this so-called army, the officers would have received a grilling from their superiors, if we had left so many bullets in those boxes – this would have meant that we had not practiced sufficiently the defence of the realm. Therefore, we were given handfuls of bullets, without any counting, and we were allowed to shoot in whatever way we wished… It really is beyond me, how we never killed anybody by accident in that superbly organised, loud and thoroughly idiotic military chaos.

On our left, there was a crumbling perimeter fence; this had a merely symbolic role. Beyond this fence, which was held together only by socialist revolutionary spirit, villagers used to take shortcuts to get into the city. A soldier in a watchtower was supposed to raise and lower a flag, depending on the absence or presence of some civilian out there. Well, he was supposed to, but often we were the first ones to notice some colourful human shape in the distance, while we were working out which completely misaligned target to aim at.

A more indirect defence of the realm also existed... It was the defence of minds that might have been exposed to something different to what they were supposed to be indoctrinated with. Hence, travel to the West was something that only privileged, trusted people could undertake – or certain trusted celebrities who the country wished to "export".

It is difficult to explain nowadays, that a kid like me truly believed that he would never see what lay beyond the Iron Curtain. After all, even the fellow communist countries were difficult to experience for real.

Our passports were not really ours. The Securitate kept them, and released them to us only when we applied to travel to the neighbouring Hungary. We had to fill in many forms with the details of several generations of our family.

My parental grandfather had been labelled a *bourgeois*, because he had employed people in his little company before the Second World War; they had been hand-polishing antique furniture before the Communists came to power. Still, until the mid-eighties, we managed to get our passports every few years, so we were able to pay short visits to folks on the other side of the border.

Hungary used to produce, print, and import many things that were banned in Romania. If we bought any of the banned books or records, then our return trip turned into a voyage of fear - but never into one of guilt.

Then, from the mid-80s onwards, our applications started to be declined. We thought this was due to the general tightening of the regime during those years. However, after the Revolution, it turned out that the real reason was a Securitate file about my Dad. He used to watch his mouth, except when he went on his fishing trips with his trusted colleagues... One of them was an informer – ironically, he was of Hungarian ethnicity, and my Dad had trusted him the most.

Nothing happened to us, thankfully – but one tangible consequence was that were no longer allowed to travel abroad, not even to communist Hungary. Hungarian ethnics were anyway more "watched" than the Romanian population... After all, we had access to Hungarian media that was full of infinitely more outspoken and dangerous ideas, and they were often criticising what was happening to ethnic minorities in Romania.

Back in those days, one had to apply even for a few minutes of international phone calls; simply dialling another country was impossible. We used to wait hours and hours until a woman eventually rang us and established the call. Then she listened in on the whole conversation we had with our relatives in Hungary. She also used to intervene regularly, just to tell us how many minutes of the call remained.

People used to wait 8-10 years to get a phone line installed in their homes – not because of technical or logistical difficulties; direct contact between people separated by various distances, in the days before the arrival of internet and mobile phones, was not desirable. Networking, of any kind, could endanger the regime, and their definition of the defence of the realm...

XII. BREATH

My asthma, first diagnosed at the age of four, allowed me to build a detailed picture about the inner workings of the Romanian health service in the 1970s and '80s.

The presence of a chemical plant in our town probably affected asthma statistics, as cases sharply increased in the '70s... I had the dubious honour of being selected as one of the five most serious chronic cases in the county. This also meant selections for experimental treatments of new drugs that some doctors managed to bring from abroad.

I am still convinced that there is no act more organic than inhaling and exhaling air; I still think that nothing scares a kid more than failing to perform that simple act. Maybe I am biased...

The attacks brought an inability to exhale. I used to fill up gradually with stale air; my sides were hurting, it felt as if every rib wanted to bend more and more while I was taking tiny gulps of air. Trying to exhale was a real effort; I painfully tried to squeeze used air out of my lungs, always hoping that at least the same tiny quantity of fresh air would make it successfully into my lungs... Scariest was the knowing that the amount of precious air would keep decreasing and decreasing...

I heard my wheezing sounds like those made by some broken bagpipe or some screwed up vacuum cleaner... so when will it either stop completely or just be done with this crap for good… but oh God sometimes tens of minutes sometimes a few hours of this crap so would I *can* I wait that long can a body suffocate itself oh can it be that that stupid yes probably it can but don't get scared that just makes it worse you know that well and it squeezes that damn chest more and I'm so sweaty my shirt is sticking to my body as if I need anything more to confine and grab and squeeze my chest oh shit this is so stupid I would do anything *anything* in the world to have one deep breath again please just do something I really don't care just end this one way or the other…

Before doctors could start prescribing potent imported inhalers, my Dad used to lift my little, light, wheezing body and he walked around in the room with me, talking to me, trying to soothe my terrified mind at least, since he could not do anything about my body.

Whenever I actually turned blue as the damn thing really began to starve my body of oxygen, then it was time to give up and call an ambulance – the bringer of the cortisone shot…

Once, the whole mare caught me while we were at the mountain resort of Tusnad, sent there by my doctor. Sea and mountains, those great opposites of our country, were seen as natural cures for the condition. The Black Sea was too far away from us, so the Carpathian Mountains around Transylvania were the closer and easier solution.

Before allergy tests, capable of identifying the triggers of the asthma attacks, could be imported, we could not figure out the pattern of what was causing the more severe attacks. Unfortunately for me, the motel in Tusnad had luscious duck feather pillows – and bang, there I was, blue again, age seven, skinny and hence fortunately very light, in a mountain village with only one very sleepy doctor, and not one working phone in the motel…

So, my Dad lifted me into his arms; his routine was perfectly polished by then. He managed to run half a kilometre with me to the doctor, woke him up, and I received my hydrocortisone shot that, as usual, solved everything.

I have never talked about the psychobabble side of all this to anyone, but I am still very sure that it does something to a kid. After all, I lived in constant primal fear of my own body.

I hated it.

I hated it not because of some contemporary, and stupid, body image problem induced by some male models or celebrities. I wish I had today's usual teenage angst about looks, weight and, oh yes, muscles.

It was a *lot* simpler in my case; I simply feared and hated my body, full stop.

The bastard could just randomly turn me into a sweaty, quivering, panicking, and, above all, desperately wheezing bundle of a few anatomic parts - just two tiny lungs, some ribs and one tortured mind. My mind was trying to hide from the fear, then the discomfort, and then the physical pain that was unleashed on it by two small pink bags filled with stale air.

I cannot quite describe the feeling of an asthma attack gradually going away.

It was… as if a very heavy monster with a *huge* arse was standing up slowly, leaving my chest that he had used as a comfortable sofa on which he fidgeted randomly… It was a priceless feeling to be slowly taking deeper and deeper breaths, to be able to push out the trapped air and gradually replace it with life… It really *was* physical pleasure. It was as if some door had opened inside me; it really was a strange and basic version of Heaven.

As soon as I was able to control all this terrifyingly random mess with imported inhalers, I felt like an animal tamer, whenever that nasty monster jumped on my chest in school or on the street. Prior to that, only some steroid-based pills had helped, but they were very slow acting - so I used walk home very slowly, while my breathing was getting worse and worse.

Doctors had nothing logical to offer me as a long-term solution; the local specialists had been decades behind the Western knowledge. One must remember that this was before the age of the internet, before doctors could attend international conferences… Still, some drugs they did manage to get their hands on, and very, very few specialists were allowed to have some contact with the West.

Eventually, when I was eleven years old, we found such a doctor; he was, for some reason, allowed to travel abroad a lot. He managed to bring back heaps of interesting stuff – and one day, during my guinea pig phase, he could show me red spots on my forearm – the results of a modern allergy test. Finally, somebody was able to tell us that there was logic and a pattern to all of that nasty mess.

So, the doctor's orders went like this: stay away from house dust, flowers and feathers; if autumnal humid weather comes, don't walk too fast, don't run, don't be a *kid*, just take care and have the inhaler, the pills and some water on you at all times. Do not use the *Berotec* inhaler too soon, as it does things to your heart, too – plus, it is addictive...

My mother laughed when she heard the latter. She assured the doctor: there would not be any problems with my over-reliance on the drug. She knew that I would always endure the attacks for at least an hour, and if the monster after all that time was still using my chest as a sofa, then and only then I would consider using the inhaler.

I inherited a lot of deep-seated hope, combined with endurance, from my mother... I cannot explain any other reason for my torturing of myself for tens of minutes as the attack was clearly getting worse, not immediately resorting to that little can of magic. After a couple of puffs, it made the heavy monster lift his fat arse off my chest and run away.

After I grew up, this self-torturing variant of hope plus endurance came handy for so many other things that, albeit located outside my body, were similarly nasty and unpredictable.

I was used in long medical trials, too, whenever some asthma specialist managed to get some new drug from abroad. Drugs like *Intal* were first tried on us in the entire county – gosh, what an honour, right? Our small group of chronic asthma sufferers had to administer it, and then we had to fill long evaluation sheets to record how we felt during the trial.

Still, the only thing that ever produced long-term positive results for me was desensitisation, a therapy that is controversial to this day. The doctor, who had performed the allergy test on me, embarked on a two-year long journey with a few of his most severe patients.

Therefore, when I turned thirteen, I noticed that after the very long series of injections I was finally able to stay indoors whenever my Dad was vacuuming in the house. I was able to walk among trees and flowers in the spring. I could sleep on feather pillows for the first time in my life...

The allergies were gone; all that remained were random, still very annoying, but milder asthma attacks that had no such clear triggers. These attacks were brought on sometimes by wet weather, sometimes by fog, often just by laughing and exerting my lungs too much. Ah, the irony... The comedies and cartoons that helped me escape from Ceausescu's weird Universe could trigger the asthma attacks in cinemas, so I always had to have the inhaler on me. That tiny thing allowed me to laugh freely.

So, yes, I had used potent chemicals - not to induce, but to *enable* happy times.

This stubborn, mostly physical effort-triggered asthma nonsense meant that during primary, secondary and high school I was medically exempt from any physical effort... Hence, I was frail and tiny, a biped asthmatic misery, pale and with the posture of a question mark kicked up its backside, as some described it.

I only realised much later that some ad-hoc treatments, prescribed back then with the best knowledge Romanian medicine was allowed to possess, had been downright stupid. For example, long course of steroid pills was meant to suppress the allergic reactions that were triggering my asthma attacks. Of course, these pills steam hammered my immune system and I caught myriad infections.

However, among all the things prescribed by the doctors, swimming was one thing I really enjoyed. It helped in my strengthening of thoracic muscle; with the arrival of inhalers, I was advised to inhale a puff of that magic substance before swim. Still, since my lung capacity was lame, I had to take several long breaks even if my arms and tiny muscles could have continued to propel me in the water. It was frustrating to have to leave the pool several times, in order to catch my breath even when my body was not tired at all.

Still, that was a rather normal sensation of being out of breath. In a way, it was a relief compared to the visits from that obese monster, which used to accommodate itself comfortably on my chest to read some new edition of 'Sadism Weekly'.

At least the medical exemptions had given me a solid reason to avoid certain communist 'homage' marathons. The medical issues saved me from compulsory National Service, too. The medical requirement for getting out of military service was to produce an asthma attack under supervision, while one stayed in a military hospital for a few weeks.

The communist military machine used to suck in anybody who was able to function at a basic level; it sometimes killed or, in fortunate cases, hospitalised lads with severe medical conditions. Therefore, the probability of I ending up drafted with even severe asthma were pretty much 100%, but an unforeseeable side effect of a medical decision altered the odds in my favour. The doctors' recommendation to have me begin school at age seven instead of six, because of my asthma and my general physical state, has modified my personal timeline in vital ways.

If I had started school at age six, then I would have been doing my military service during the overthrowing of the Ceausescu regime in December 1989. I turned 18 in the summer of 1989, and I finished high school on that very summer. Thus, I would have joined the army on that autumn, regardless of whether I managed to get into a University or not. The only difference was that military service lasted one year for students, and one and a half years for those who did not go to University.

"Education, education, education", repeated the regime ad nauseam - and they certainly made sure that they educated the kids to become robots who forgot most of what they had learnt before University. The lads used to return to the real world quite dazed and confused, after a year spent in a parallel, absurd, and militarised Universe - and only then, they could continue their education.

However, as I had started school with a one-year delay, I only finished high school after the Revolution. Hence, I began my University studies in 1990 - and this altered my life path completely. In 1990, a shorter military service was introduced, and this had to be completed *after* one finished University. In addition, the drafting criteria were relaxed; so, based on my huge medical file and a detailed series of tests, I went through the process rather smoothly in 1995. I ended up with a priceless piece of paper, which stated that I was not apt for military service.

Nevertheless, if that metallic green and grey mechanised world had swallowed me in 1995, then that would have happened five years after the drawn-out, bloody and tragic armed conflict between the army and the removed Leader's secret police. That fight raged for many weeks all over the country; they were shooting each other in the forests, on the mountains, even on the streets – often snipers were pitted against poorly equipped and inexperienced teenage soldiers.

I can thank my asthma, which led to a one-year delay in my schooling, the fact that I never had to aim a weapon at a living being. More importantly, nobody managed to aim one at me on the streets of Bucharest or wherever we would have ended up as soldiers.

To paddle back to the topic of the Romanian healthcare system, well, the vision was as grand as all of Ceausescu's visions were. Only in my hometown, apart from the specialist clinics, they had built several polyclinics. The one they had built on the hillside, next to a military shooting ground and a new cemetery, was notorious for its labyrinthine internal layout. People kept getting lost all the time, and we successfully managed to do that several times with my parents.

The cemetery kept on expanding; by the late 1980s, the graves ended up just a couple of hundred yards away from the back of the vast building - exactly behind the intensive care and emergency departments. I often wondered what those patients thought and felt when they looked out the window.

A lot of the staff's interest in, and care for, the patients was fuelled by regular envelopes containing banknotes, sometimes by small bags with hard-to-get imported coffee or chocolate. Otherwise, as we knew all too well (nobody had been exactly bursting with health in our family), one could have literally died in a corner... and nobody would have cared for a while.

The regime was convinced that even humble viruses composed of just a strand of DNA, not capable of subversive imperialist views, had to be ideologically scrutinised. Certain diseases and conditions could not exist in the glorious society we were building; they were the diseases that could only exist in the West.

Therefore, HIV could not exist in Romania. The AIDS that it caused could not exist. Any doctor who dared to report such cases was to face the *Securitate*... Any doctor who got his or her hands on test kits for such banned diseases was in even bigger trouble - because that was seen as a deliberate subversive act.

Would one watch some patient die of a banned disease? Would one fake the medical reports? Would one make those state just some out-of-control pneumonia, or some mysterious organ failures, or whatever? Would one make waves and maybe try to do something for diagnosing those conditions officially? Latter would have been a political crime, with all its consequences...

The blood used for transfusions could not be tested for such germs. Although, for example, HIV cases were still very rare, one simply had to hope that the blood received during an operation was something lifesaving, and not than life terminating.

However, by the late 1980s, the number of HIV-positive children skyrocketed... A few doctors, who believed that the Hippocratic Oath was more important than their own physical and financial wellbeing, had been testing for HIV and produced reports that were aired anonymously on *Radio Free Europe* and *Voice of America*.

It did not matter whether those figures were perhaps exaggerated by such mass media, because the facts remained: there was a hot and deadly wind blowing, to use the words of Laurie Anderson somewhat inexactly - but people, who were able to notice it, could not say anything. Worse, they could not *do* anything.

Ceausescu's alternate Universe was a place where classic philosophical subjective reality reigned. If one did not know about something, it did not exist.

Not only germs were subject to ideological branding during those years; mental health, too, was a major concern for the regime. Certain psychiatric diagnoses were simply banned.

Depression was ruining lives, leading to suicides - but it could only occur in the oh-so-decadent West, of course. It was something that only a person like Sue Ellen in the *Dallas* TV series could suffer from, as she was drowning in her gold-plated misery. In contrast, we lived in a positive society; we were building a luminous world... except when electricity was cut for several hours...

Evil, after it had roamed Romania's mountains and plains for centuries, evolved. It was no longer mythical, and it was immune to light. This evil was a rational and well-planned one.

This rational planning had meant that my paternal grandmother, with a stomach cancer that had been misdiagnosed for many months, used to wait for at least twenty minutes for the ambulance, whenever the pain struck her down. The ambulance station was very close to us, a mere five-minute walk away - but anybody above the age of sixty had lowest priority. Even if the paramedics had nothing else to do, they simply had to delay their help.

Old people were simply a burden – I still wonder, whether the regime's hate toward them was at least partly caused by the fact that they had seen what the world was like before communism...

Stalin had executed many, even the soldiers, who had seen the West. Instead, Ceausescu made sure that the older generation had an increased chance of expiring as early as possible. With them, the memories of another world died gradually.

XIII. VISION

Darkness was not all bad – it used to create the ambience in which I could install my own imaginary, very personal movie screen, to turn on my own little projector of the mind.

Radio plays made me imagine the characters, the scenes and vista. Reading was a delicacy, a true feast, since my senses were not tied to anything pre-fabricated – everything was built from nothing, in my mind's movie sets.

Oh yes, there were films, too - classics of Italian, French and English cinema, some American films (mostly cowboy movies, a few old thrillers), many black-and-white movies or often monochrome copies of the colour originals... Therefore, among all that cultural starvation instated by the regime, one actually had the chance to grow up while watching great cinematic masterpieces, but also many entertaining old gems...

I devoured countless old films with my parents. We used to go to the cinema several times a week; we checked out the six cinemas in my hometown, we hunted celluloid memories of other worlds.

We watched classics that ranged from *Some Like It Hot* to Antonioni's *Blow-Up*, *Zorba the Greek* to *Kramer vs. Kramer*, *What's up Doc* to *Gunfight at O.K. Corral*... Even if I often did not understand the *tours de force* of Buñuel or Antonioni or Godard, they made me feel, think, *sense* - in a world where, outside the walls that encased darkness, a beam of light, and bodiless shapes on a screen, there was no much magic....

Sounds odd, but I am grateful for the screen giants like Mastroianni, Delon, Cardinale, Montand, Belmondo, Funès, the Hepburns and many others, because they had shaped my image of what a real film star meant.

Unfortunately for our current, much hyped, hordes of "stars", if all the kids had watched, in a state of beautifully aching daze and reverence, the pure light & shadow glory unleashed on screen by true movie legends, then those kids would not be able to admire mass-produced Hollywood mediocrity...

Funnily, this is why Ceausescu's cultural starvation plans had backfired.

The carefully enforced absence of beauty and humanity in our everyday life had created a dark void, where the beautiful, but painfully ephemeral flares on the cinema screens seemed even brighter. As the ancient Roman saying goes, light is brighter in the dark. We did not get hooked on Romanian films, which glorified the communist regime; instead, we became film buffs addicted the everlasting movies and genuine talents.

Sometimes, more recent films were imported, if they were deemed "educational". They bought *The Towering Inferno* probably because, in their minds, it showed how faulty things could be designed by the West – because, of course, nobody in the communist world had ever built lethal buildings...

They bought István Szabó's *Mephisto*, despite its powerful depiction of informers, opportunism and moral corruption during the Nazi regime. Maybe some subversive censors intentionally let it pass through their filter... we will never know. When we were kids, we did not care about the mental processes that took place in the censors' minds - as long as we could go and see some brand new movie.

The ticket queues were of absurd proportions – but these were not hordes of marionettes pulled to the box office by the strong strings of mega-hype. Instead, these crowds were genuinely starving for new sights – hence, the arrival of any new film from the West was a truly major event.

I admit that *Cinema Paradiso* still brings me to tears - for me, it is the only film that really captures the unique feeling of true, immense, and deep wonder that we used to experience whenever a new film arrived in our cinemas.

Nowadays, while our senses and billboards are saturated by myriad "unmissable" movies, I find it hard to explain to people just how nostalgic I feel about my childhood's movie screenings... Lights were dimmed, curtains revealed the screen's silent and inert surface, which was about to be lit up by images that were pure escapism for us; images that meant a few hours of travelling in another world...

I used to squeeze my parents' hands when the first cracks and pops came from the old speakers – these were the sure signs that, within a few seconds, amazing things would start happening on the screen...

Theatre life was not so vibrant, possibly due to more censorship. At least, our local theatre company managed to stage many classic plays. When salaries were stable, and the economy (a fictitious one of course, with absurd laws) was stable, one did not have to care about how many tickets were sold.

However, the theatres used to be full; we often had to sit on the stairs. It was another form of escapism, but... if one does not have to worry about how to attract people to the productions, then one can focus on what happens on stage. Hence, they were pouring all their energy into the acting and the staging. There was a passionate freshness in those plays; it is something that is hard to find nowadays – after the Revolution, money and funding started to matter in an entirely different way.

We had many school trips back then to other theatre and opera companies, like the famous one in Kolozsvár (i.e. Cluj).

Opera was something we only managed to see snippets of on TV, inserted between some propaganda crud... A performance of Verdi's *Un ballo in Maschera*, by a Hungarian minority opera company from Kolozsvár, vividly stayed in my memory - not just because of the higher-than-usual density of bonbons and drawing pins thrown on stage by the kids, but also due to the comedy that enfolded from the collision between languages...

That remarkable and hilarious collision was brought on by a virus, which had knocked out one a singer more effectively than the fake dagger he would have been killed by on stage. So, he was quickly replaced by whomever they could find to sing the part - and that person happened to be a Romanian singer.

For hours and hours through the great show, through my first live opera experience, everybody sang in Hungarian... except for that one person. Thus, any operatic dialogue between him and anybody else on stage was bringing us to spasms of childish laughter... The operatic Babel that unfolded on stage was also a great, albeit purely accidental, parable of the multi-ethnic reality in those years.

Inevitably, the urge not just to consume, but also to produce images had infiltrated my thoughts early on. I caught an incurable bug when my first cousin, aunt and my parents got me a 13th birthday present; it was a small box with Cyrillic characters on it.

It was my first camera: a small, fully manual, rudimentary, but brilliant Russian box of magic... a *Smena*. It fit into a larger pocket, it was lighter than any Soviet-made object of that size, hence it was atypically fragile; springs and wheels and tiny levers animated it. It also had surprisingly good lenses, and everything on it was fully adjustable.

I am, to this day, immensely grateful for that present... and for what that camera *did* to me. Nowadays, empowered with my state-of-the-art SLR cameras, bags of lenses and various gizmos, I am genuinely glad that the little *Smena* made me think and see things differently.

All I had back then was a shutter speed dial with extremely sunny, sunny, not so sunny, cloudy, and rainy pictograms, some numbers on the diaphragm dial, and a rudimentary focus ring with distances and pictograms of a portrait, a person, a group of people and then for the infinite distance setting, trees with hills... Exposure meters were very expensive, so they really were out of the question.

I had to learn many things... I learnt about contrast, about optics and depth of field. I kept wondering, until the moment the film emerged from the photo lab, how accurate my judgment of exposure times had been.

Many years later, I was sitting at a camera club's meeting in England; I had to listen with straight face to a toe-curling, pompous guest speaker, who was explaining that "only forty years of photography" could make someone accurately judge exposure... Oh, I wish I had the courage to tell him about how we learnt exposure, with a precision of half f-stop, using just our eyes and mind.

Was this, too, just one more example of how the absence of something could lead, paradoxically, to a significant gain in our lives? Less really *was* more in those days.

I installed a little film-processing lab in the bathroom, to my parents' great joy... I used to put towels in the small window and under the door, so that I could stop light getting in. We could buy chemicals imported from East Germany; these were pricey, but *über*-precise in their effects. Doctors could not tell whether those chemicals would have had any effect on my asthma - so my passion outweighed the worries.

It took some convincing, but my parents, after a few lab sessions that had no effect on me at all, did let me turn the bathroom into a chemical hazard zone from time to time. The only visible effect that it had on me was the satisfied grin on my face, which could not be erased for hours and hours - especially while I watched the drying negatives in our kitchen. This used to cost a lot less, than photo labs.

I could not have predicted how beneficial my ability to turn opaque plastic strips into a series of images would become later, when pictures of the ethnic pogrom of March 1990 had to be processed in as much secret as possible.

XIV. DREAM

In a world where streets had been monochrome scenes of struggle for physical and, above all, moral survival, the outer space was a fascinating place in our imagination. It was not a cold vacuum; instead, it was full of emotions and drama. Its vast expanse with myriad amazing worlds made the absurd tragicomedy in our daily lives seem insignificant...

Many kids were, as many are today, fans of science fiction – albeit of varying quality... I believe it was mainly a form of escapism for us. Hence, we turned our attention to a certain category of sci-fi literature that was allegorical, filled with very subversive ideas. Such ideas in any other literary setting, and even in much milder form, would have caught the attention of the censors.

We devoured subversive sci-fi literature with true hunger. However, it was difficult to get my hands on the annual *Anticipatia* almanacs, on other collections of sci-fi stories and novels.

I used to beg the woman in the tiny and narrow newspaper shop in the city centre, the one place that always ordered in a few copies of the almanac. A box of proper chocolate, a pack of real coffee used to go a long way - but all these by the '80s became just memories, so it was not so easy to think of some equally effective mini-bribe. So, I had to rely on her benevolence and on her motherly instinct. Both were triggered in her by the sight of a kid who, during the few weeks when the almanac was expected to be published, used to come every couple of days to ask whether she had received any copies yet.

My Mum used to pop in to chat to her from time to time. After the completion of each successful hunt for the sci-fi almanac, she used to bring her some sweets, or lent her some books to help with her son's compulsory reading list. We did all this for a precious thing, filled with translations of sci-fi short stories from the genre's greats - all set in oh-so-very-different worlds.

Sure, some sci-fi had been blacklisted. The authors of high quality, and often allegoric, sci-fi works had been writing about religion, spirituality, freedom of thought, all set in distant and fantastic worlds. The messages were sometimes veiled in techie mumbo-jumbo, which managed to evade the attention of the not completely stupid censors.

For example, a collection of stories entitled *No God in Cosmos* seemed to promote loudly the ideas of an atheism, which was favoured by the Party. It was wonderful irony, that at the same time the Party collaborated and financed the Romanian Orthodox church, purely because latter was a vital tool in the indoctrination of the masses. Now that apparently atheist collection of sci-fi stories was actually filled with deeply thought provoking and utterly spiritual gems from the great classics of the genre.

Thus, in the hands of writers who wanted to get dangerous ideas across, without the risk of spending a few decades in political prisons, sci-fi was a very special weapon. The power of this subversive weapon came from two aspects. On one hand, the regime loved anything scientific; in their minds, sci-fi was about the triumph of technology - after all, the communist society was, of course, on route to such greatness. On the other hand, while the regime allowed and even promoted this literature, sci-fi was *the* perfect vehicle for brilliant and dangerous social, political, and ideological messages.

Such cryptic and subversive literature became our absolute

favourite by the time we reached our mid-teen years; by then, we had read enough classic literature to be able to spot and understand metaphors and symbols.

However, some Romanian authors did get into trouble, when their works were translated and published in the West. Usually, those writers were put under observation - and this used to happen not just in Romania, but also across the communist bloc.

People like Alexandru Mironov had managed to get very friendly with the regime; so much so, that he was allowed to make short TV shows, to publish sci-fi anthologies, and to promote homegrown talent. Many of my friends hated such people, as they appeared to be opportunists. However, I think that such people were not really collaborators of the regime. If they were that, then it was inexplicable why they picked such dangerously subversive novels and stories for their publications and TV shows. Similarly, opportunism cannot explain why such people were promoting local talent like George Ceausu, or the Hungarian ethnic György Mandics, both of whom had been writing social and political sci-fi of international calibre, with extremely strong anti-totalitarian themes.

To be honest, as a teenage kid I could not care less about such alleged opportunists' affiliations or convictions, as long as every few months I could get my hands on publications that made me escape the everyday trivia. However, at the same time, such publications made me discover, and meditate on, the more subtle aspects of my rather absurd everyday reality.

I find it ironic that most of the sci-fi in today's mainstream media is terribly superficial, childish, and fully action-packed. It makes many people, who do have the sensitivity for more meaningful flights of the imagination, avoid the entire genre. I know some very literate people who would not touch a sci-fi novel with a barge pole, due to their exposure to silly TV series…

That kid of the '80s, who was reading Lem, Dick, and Bradbury, did not have much in common with a kid who is nowadays watching these silly TV series. That 1980s kid desperately needed more thought-provoking stories, in order to convince himself that there was much more possible in life, that other people believed in the same – and that such people at least had thought of entirely different, better worlds. Those worlds were always more fascinating and better than the one I used to find every morning outside our house.

It is not surprising, that after the Revolution, when suddenly one could write about anything, when there was no longer a need for expressing something powerful via hidden meanings, sci-fi literature plummeted in quality and depth. It plunged into the realm of hardcore, technological science fiction, which had no intention to tell us important things about the world we lived in.

The poetic voices have gradually disappeared; much of the new generation of "free" sci-fi writers have become slaves to sales figures. In an economy that turned so *real* in every sense of the word, money started to matter infinitely more than subtle meaning of any kind.

XV. REVOLUTION

By the end of the 1980s, the regime's suffocating measures of control had reached unbearable levels. Just when we really began to think that nothing would ever change, that we were stuck in that bizarre world with no chance of exiting from it, the Revolution came...

It started as a small, stubborn demonstration led by Laszlo Tokes, a Hungarian reformed pastor in Temesvár (or Timisoara in Romanian). His protest action steadily grew, began to spread, and by 19 December 1989 it ignited most of the Transylvanian cities. This sudden heat wave then crossed the Carpathian Mountains, reached Bucharest - and permanently burned its mark into history.

We heard via the banned radio stations what was happening in Timisoara, and that it spread to other towns. Still, it came as a surprise to us that an evening protest in our city centre attracted a few dozen, then hundreds, then tens of thousands of people... When the protest reached that size, gunshots were heard; seven people were shot by the army... Later we heard, and then felt, the rumble of the tanks; the old streets and houses vibrated to that infernal, universally recognisable sound of Power...

On the following day, we were just idling after lunch. We heard our neighbour shout: turn on the TV, turn on the TV! In the middle of the day, instead of the usual nothingness of static, there was TV transmission coming from the capital's main newsroom...

However, the people on the TV screen were not the usual newsreaders, who on the previous evening had been busily denying that a Ceausescu-led rally in Bucharest had drowned in shouting and general chaos. Instead, we saw some people in sweaters and torn shirts, sweaty and out of breath, shouting and wildly gesticulating in front of the camera... I cannot remember what they were shouting; in the shock of it, we only grasped that it meant the *end* of something that we could not imagine ever ending. The army had switched sides and it, with the vast crowds on the streets, put an end to it all.

22 December 1989 brought euphoria, tides of people on the streets; it brought smashing and tearing of portraits, ripping of the communist emblem from the national flag, which, with a whole in its centre, later became the symbol of the Romanian Revolution.

I remember the layers of smashed Ceausescu portraits; their glass was covering the streets of our town centre. People were ecstatically destroying with their hands, teeth and feet the symbols of the so-called Golden Era; they were destroying the books about the Party, endlessly shouting "Down with Ceausescu!", "Down with communism!"...

Indeed, the dominant direction that the old regime's symbols were taking was *down*.

Everything was spiralling downwards during those few days, down into a maelstrom of mass annihilation. Statues, portraits, display panels, signs, flags, and furniture were thrown from the rooms of the former Power into the streets. All were devoured by the insatiable, noisy, but benevolent, giant myriapod, which wanted to gobble up every crumb of what was gone for good - hopefully.

Not much later, after the army had finally won the battle against the still resisting forces of the Securitate, after He and She were hastily executed, when there was nothing left to smash, to trample on and to rip to pieces, came the calmness of gathering strength.

A calm, after all that tearing and ripping; a tranquillity of catching one's breath after all that shouting and running and waving and laughing, laughing, finally properly laughing...

Then came a quiet resting, after all that gathering and hugging... and, eventually, came the question: what next?

I really felt strange after those few, surreal, burning-hot winter days. Christmas was coming, the first free Christmas. We could not put much under the tree – but, after all those years of not having much, we suddenly felt that we had *everything*. It was not a tangible everything - just a plain, but almost incomprehensible, vastness of everything.

I would have exchanged all my subsequent Christmases, with their ever-increasing piles of tangible goodies and tangible realities, for that one Christmas of invisible everything...

In many ways, that Revolution was exactly like an explosion... It had instantaneously destroyed a world of musts and don'ts, and, behind its expanding shockwave, it created a momentary vacuum of what-nows and where-tos. Then, that vacuum sopped up everything, indiscriminately; it filled the void with confusing multitudes and superficial plenitudes.

The whirlwinds of the debris that the vacuum had absorbed from the West slowly quieted down. Over the course of too many years, all that blustery chaos sedimented into a new reality that was showing some degree of sense.

After all the constraining and restraining pressure that had been acting on every surface of our small world, 1989 removed all those pressure forces. Hence, everything around us not just expanded, but many things, no longer pushed under the ground by those forces, burst to the surface... Latent tensions, antagonisms, and hidden evil liberated themselves. We knew fascism only from books, but we were about to experience it on our streets. We only knew the Mafia from films, but we were about to see something similar take over every inch of our new reality.

Still, we went from a Universe governed by simple and predictable Newtonian mechanics to something that was ruled by complex and confusing quantum mechanics.

Before the changes, we were limited to very few specific choices and possibilities. There had been no fashion trends and fads; no music charts, as there was only the music we could get our hands on via fellow music fans. Only a few "brands" had existed ... so we used to make up our own mind about what we liked, without the marketing hype we experience nowadays.

Then, suddenly, all the rigid limitations, but, crucially, also the very few certainties of our existence, vanished. These were demolished, shot by a firing squad, torn, ripped up in one big, shouting, flag-waving, and bullet-dodging bang.

We used to have only some quasi-underground religious and spiritual life, but suddenly everything was rushing into the vacuum that was created behind the still reverberating bang. From Buddhism to Satanism to New Age, all the possible religions, sects, and quasi-religious fads were setting up their tents, metaphorically and literally, on our streets.

Teenagers began to gather in half-demolished church buildings, setting up satanic sects, trying out what they saw on some album covers and concert snapshots. One of my friends wanted to travel to Tibet; he wanted to abandon his education, and he was planning to ignore his upcoming Baccalaureate. The most distant and exotic lands, sights, thoughts, and imagined realities suddenly became irresistibly attractive – and they all seemed reachable.

We used to have one haircut and one uniform; suddenly, we had all the fashion trends from all over the world. Kids started to go to school in customised leather jackets covered with metal chains and with other heavy metal rock symbolism. By the summer of 1990, most of them ended up wearing ultra-long hairdos, segregating into groups, flaunting their new "identities" with their clothing.

When the first Nike shop opened in Bucharest, the first shop of genuine Western sports equipment, a student colleague of mine, who had already very rich parents, bought a return flight to the capital – just so that he could be among the very first genuine Nike-wearing lads...

We used to have desperately few newspapers and magazines; after the Revolution, we saw an explosion of zillions of magazines printed about everything... These were copied and put together from other magazines, news, photos, articles, translations of articles.

Music was pouring out of shops; all sorts of companies appeared overnight, producing and selling top-quality pirate copies of many albums. These companies and shops started to sell cassettes, and later they moved on to pirated CDs. Tens of thousands of films on pirated VHS tapes were pouring out of other, equally suddenly appearing, stores. Some of these shops were installed in the owners' houses, and cardboard signs used to direct people to these new musical or visual heavens. Video clubs appeared; there was one installed even in the puppet theatre on our street. These were boasting a large TV on stage, and everybody was queuing for tickets.

The few hours of propaganda TV programs were replaced with national TV channels that stayed on air round the clock, broadcasting absolutely anything and everything they could find. More and more local TV stations followed, broadcasting endlessly from often-improvised tiny studios. These turned the quiet ether, which had only been perturbed by loud propaganda before the Revolution, into something quite stormy.

During the first few months of 1990, before anybody even remotely thought of copyright laws, these stations used to flood the ethers with broadcasts of personal videotapes of films, concerts, shows, and sights that most people could only fantasise about before. I recall those first few days of non-stop broadcasting, an insane storm of visions and sounds, an electronic flood that was satisfying an immeasurable hunger...

People suddenly discovered new needs. New hungers. New drives. New obsessions.

An asexual society turned into a porn party. Suddenly, nudist riverside areas turned up, adult magazines covered the newsagents' windows; soft-core films were shown on TV in the middle of the day. Eventually the Romanian Orthodox church freaked out, and tried to introduce some film rating system with watersheds. The somewhat hilarious result of their action was that adult films were shown after the watershed, but then they were repeated during daytime on the following day. It was just one example of how Romania began to apply new rules in a characteristically illogical manner.

One political Party was replaced by all the possible parties that talked about all the possible and ludicrously impossible things – new thoughts, new terminology, new sides, new promises, new ambitions, new contradictions... and new lies.

The few shops of the communist past, with their depressingly empty shelves, exploded into new, long rows of busy shops.

People were selling anything and everything; they cut doors and display windows in the walls of their houses or ground floor flats. At first, most of these were selling food and drink, then cigarettes and flowers, then clothing, then imported second-hand stuff.

The dream of making money, *real* money and not just some symbolic currency in a symbolic economy, completely overtook people's minds. Pyramid schemes flourished, direct and multi-level marketing schemes arrived. That former *nothing* began to change, with dizzying speed, into *everything* - indiscriminate, unfiltered, uncensored, and uncontrolled everything.

Going back to school, after that special and surreal Christmas, continuing my final year in high school, preparing for the gruelling baccalaureate and the even scarier entrance exams for the University I was planning to study at... now that was a truly strange experience. It replaced the surreal euphoria of those few revolutionary days of December with a new version of reality I could not have imagined before.

It was a new reality, in which the torn flags and overturned statues could not magically erase all the realities of the Era that had ended just before Christmas.

The most difficult few weeks were those of the realisation that the great myriapod, which had devoured on our streets everything that was old, had to dismember itself. It had to split into individual particles... We all had to come to terms with the new daily reality.

People were hoping for new politicians who could speak the truth. However, those who turned up on the TV screen in the early days, those days of euphoria, slowly eroded pixel by pixel; they were replaced by a new breed of hypocrites. The National Salvation Front, with Ion Iliescu, became the most despised neo-communist outfit.

People of ethnic minority backgrounds hoped that all of their fundamental rights would finally become reality. However, just three and a half months after the Revolution, a bloody pogrom came to the streets of my hometown; it was a reminder that freedom for us would always mean a continued struggle for basic rights. One still hopes that the orchestrated pogrom we endured after 15 March 1990 will not be triggered again by the fascist elements of the new Romanian political scene. The extreme right flourished in 1990, hate spiralled out of control, and freedom to some meant that they could do anything to anyone...

A painful introduction to the new democracy and freedom was that our high school became one of the main targets of the new Romanian extreme right, which had set up headquarters in my hometown. It was called *Vatra Romaneasca*, i.e. Romanian hearth.

Instead of spending our last months in that school with quiet preparations for the Baccalaureate and the University entrance exams, we had Romanian far right demonstrations around the school and on its corridors... A few times, we literally ended up under siege; we had to block the imposing gates of the school with benches we brought from the gymnasium.

There are countless accounts of what happened after 15 March 1990 in my hometown, during the pogrom organised by the extreme right. We first heard the trucks that drove past our house; these were filled with peasants, whom the extremists brought in from mountain villages like Hodac. We did not know yet what the noise meant; but that marked the start of a few very long days.

Those were days of smashed Hungarian offices and businesses, beaten up Hungarians filling the A&E departments, demonstrations on the streets that turned into fights. The police and the army actively took part in the ethnically polarised beatings. From the real statistics gathered by paramedics and emergency hospital departments, it was very clear who started what and who beat up whom...

Andras Suto, the internationally renowned playwright and ethnic minority voice lost one eye, and almost his life, too, in the pogrom; he was beaten to a pulp in his own office. We only saw the aftermath, when we eventually ventured outside the school walls to contemplate the smashed up offices, layers of glass that covered everything, the chaos of documents, office furniture, objects from smashed shop windows...

Naturally, those sights triggered flashbacks of the Revolution; but this was just a literally bloody mess, one caused by latent ultra-nationalistic emotions. These emotions, kept under the surface of a forcefully "homogenised" society during the Ceausescu regime, had erupted with full force.

The same black, slimy extremism re-surfaced many more times after that, but not with such force. Like many primordial, well, primitive emotions that used to burst into our new reality during those early months, nationalist extremism, too found calmer and more effective ways to permeate the layers of our new society.

Some of us, equipped with small cameras, took pictures of the pogrom's aftermath; we ran like hell whenever we were spotted shooting moments of the pogrom... In the face of various claims that surfaced in the media and propaganda afterwards, I still have to ask: if the new local and national leaders were telling the truth, then why was police chasing us and everyone who tried to take pictures on those streets? Tanks were again stationed on our streets...

The pogrom was presented in the media as something organised and carried out by the Hungarian ethnic minority against the Romanian majority... Such distortion of the anyway well-known reality was simply tragicomic. The new manipulators forgot that they lived in a world where, within hours of the start of the pogrom, foreign media and countless reporters descended on the scene. The police and army did not dare to touch them, but they were suppressing any local amateur or professional armed with cameras and tape recorders.

We were labelled barbarians, invaders, and vandals from the hordes of Genghis Khan. These lessons in history would have been, in any other circumstance, quite interesting from a comedian's viewpoint, but we kind-of lost our sense of humour.

The simple fact remains that after the 15 March 1990 peaceful commemorations of the Hungarian martyrs of the 1848-1849 Revolution, a pogrom followed.

We could hold the first commemoration of the martyrs since the communist's rise to power, we had flowers and speeches and colours of the Hungarian flag deposited on the graves by delegates from Hungary... On the following day we had Romanian peasants storming the city, all of them brought by well-organised trucks and determined to beat up anybody who talked in a different language...

Those savages, simply there is no other word for describing them, possessed no knowledge of the local historic and ethnic realities. As it turned out later, they were told that Hungarian tanks had invaded Transylvania and that local Hungarian population had plotted to hand over that land to the country it once belonged to. The creativity of the fascist mind was not surprising to us, but the fertile soil on which their insanely far-fetched inventions fell did surprise us. Over time, the extremists got infinitely better at this, in comparison with those early post-Revolutionary opportunists, who used the stirred-up ethnic turbulence for their own short-term political goals.

It felt as if time had been compressed; social transformations, good and bad ones, which normally would have taken years to unfold, occurred in the timespan of just a few weeks or months... All seemed to be hastened and over-stimulated by that Revolutionary zeal.

Reality in Romania, when it came to sensitive political or ethnic issues, was still subject to the same cover-ups and distortions as it had always been during Ceausescu's reign.

When eventually the pogrom had ended, and the tanks had slowly disappeared from the city centre, the Hungarian population of my hometown and of the surrounding villages went on a well-organised, peaceful demonstration... We are stubborn people indeed; I guess this had helped us to survive all those centuries during which virtually everybody had tried to erase us from the face of the Earth.

The huge silent march was surreal. Imagine the sight of more than one hundred thousand Hungarian ethnic people, moving slowly, in completely silence, with a lit candle in one hand and a Bible in the other. The Romanian media showed only a small group of a few thousand people, the very last part of the procession. Reality in Romania remained a subjective one...

There were provocateurs, too, who tried to infiltrate the crowd, but stupidly wore different armbands - so the immune reaction of the slowly walking giant expelled them. I recall sarcastic questions from the sidewalks, as people were asking us in Romanian who had died... Nothing was attempted by the police or the army; by then, the city was swarming with foreign media people and there was too much publicity.

The whole mare of those days was the first major sign of the fact that many important things would not change in that country. Even now, after it had joined the EU, the country is still incapable of facing its distant or its recent past...

The politically exploited, chauvinistic historical inventions of professor *Daicoviciu* about the origins of the Romanians are still very much kept alive. Romanians are the direct descendants of the Dacians and Romans, with a continuous history in Transylvania since the Dacians – this was a theory that even the author renounced in his later life, as it was so fundamentally disconnected from mountains of contrary evidence. Still, his defunct theory serves the same political interests against any ethnic minority (especially in Transylvania and especially against Hungarians) as it used to do during Ceausescu's regime.

This theory is still being used as a political weapon. It was remarkable, that communist schoolbooks had claimed that 2% of Romanian words came from the Dacian language. It is quite an astonishing precision, and the pinnacle of absurdity - since not a single inscription in Dacian language exists, and no Roman text either about the language of one tiny cluster of comparatively primitive people who they have indiscriminately conquered during Trajan's time.

Small circles of sane historians began to demand a proper revision of history. The problem is that the glorious past, literally invented during Ceausescu's regime, is easier to accept than the darker, often very banal, or even humiliating, truths... Therefore, nothing changes, and nothing will change, until that nation cures its politically convenient and well-exploited delusions of grandeur. It is obvious, when something becomes a dogma: it is when one can no longer have any rational debate or discussion about a subject...

There are lot darker things, too – things still fused with the very fabric of the Romanian society, and only surfacing from time to time in subtle forms. It is not so much the ludicrous presence of Dacian kings among the Top 100 Great Romanians, as voted by the TV viewers in 2006... Nor it is the transformation of Hungarian kings, who had been rulers of Transylvania, into historical figures of Romanian origin... The more worrying aspects are the re-evaluations of Romanian history's certain characters. The presence of Ion Antonescu, the fascist leader of Romania during WW2, at No. 6 position on that chart is a subtler sign. He was "re-evaluated" after the Revolution, and almost had a statue erected in my hometown.

However, not only the fascist Antonescu made it onto the list of greatest Romanians. *Codreanu* also turned up, as a very decent No. 22. He had been the founder and leader of the *Iron Guard*, the Romanian fascist paramilitary organisation that had been responsible during WW2 for countless atrocities and assassinations, including those of writers and thinkers...

Fascism, in its current expression, in the shape of very successful organisations and parties, with downright spine-chilling characters filling the TV screens, is alive and well in Romania... Its heyday is still remembered with warm nostalgia, as shown by such lists of Top 100 and Top 10 great Romanians voted by the public...

Nevertheless, extremism existed and continues to exist on the other "side", too. The Hungarian minority's militant nationalists have sometimes caused more damage than some of the Romanian extremists have. Whenever the former have stirred up just-about-to-settle dust in the always-tense relationships between the minority and the majority, the everyday Hungarian and Romanian people, who just wanted to co-exist normally without the manipulation coming from both sides, were left to deal with the repeatedly escalated tensions.

Whenever one analyses the various manifestations of the extremists on both sides, it is difficult not to feel as if one is looking at a chicken-and-egg problem. Action and reaction have become so blurred together, that they are hard to separate.

However, exactly because of this rather amorphous mess, militant extremists with personal agendas are unforgivable. Romanian politicians do what they have always done, *divide et impera* is a very old and still very well working principle. It works every time they need votes, or need to further their power games in Transylvania and elsewhere, too. This does not remove the responsibility from Hungarian activists, authors, or politicians, though.

Whenever certain extreme right parties, ordinary individuals or public figures from Hungary travel across the border with the sole purpose to wreak havoc, as they have done in demonstrations, at football matches and at other events, they are damaging the fragile and always-tense relationships the locals have to live with. The only thing that certain Hungarian extreme right "emissaries" achieved with their violent, in more fortunate cases just provocative, acts was to make the lives of the locals more difficult.

However, Transylvanian ethnic minority personalities have resorted to the same methods, sometimes with milder intentions. My hometown, where the memory of the 1990 events is still very vivid, was turned recently into a stage prop for the political power battles of certain circles, which were based in three other Transylvanian counties. In order to further their agenda, they organized mass demonstrations in my hometown, demanding the independence of those three counties. The objective itself is not questionable, since administrative autonomy has been a recurrent and valid subject of discussion, but the means of militants putting their messages across are.

Once again, whilst diplomatic and normal political methods aimed at achieving such goals fail due to Romanian nationalism and Bucharest's resistance to any idea of decentralisation of power, the only people who actually feel the effects of the various provocative acts are the locals… Those effects are, invariably, negative ones…

XVI. POWER

After the changes, it took sixteen years for the files of the Securitate to be declassified, even if not completely. There was considerable resistance from the individuals who were occupying then, on the eve of the country's joining of the EU, the seats of political power.

However, they were not the only ones who resisted; some clergy was even more scared of the revelations. Unfortunately, some files on the exact nature of the relationship between the Securitate and the Romanian Orthodox Church remain secret.

This is hardly surprising, because that particular Church had been playing a vital role in Ceausescu's regime - and it had greatly benefited from such collaboration. It still benefits from the current relationship with the new powers; in blatant contrast with the deplorable investments in health, in education, and in basic infrastructure, it still receives vast funds for the building of thousands of churches and cathedrals.

Even the Romanian press and social media have become outspoken against the state funds diverted to this Church, and the excesses and corrupt dealings of the latter. Still, while the Orthodox Church is building places of worship anywhere it possibly can, it is still refusing to hand back to the Romanian Greco-Catholic church the assets taken from latter during the former regime...

Thus, when at least some of the Securitate's files finally saw the light of day, archbishops, patriarchs, and countless "ordinary" Orthodox priests were revealed as informers and collaborators of the Securitate. They, together with the politicians, even senators and members of the post-communist Governments who turned up on these pages, had had a very different choice to make when compared to that of our neighbour, a florist woman's husband.

He had been presented in the 1970s with a simple dilemma: the physical destruction of him and his family, or just slow moral destruction by becoming an informer. I would not have liked to be presented with such a choice - but many informers, unfortunately for them, had been forced to make such a difficult and questionable decision.

In contrast, many of the key personalities, who were still occupying comfortable positions in the post-1989 circles of power, had made the same choice out of opportunism and without any pressure. It was easy to follow in the new Romania how the shady characters of the former regime, the ones who were quietly benefiting from their spinelessness and opportunism, rapidly became the new high society.

Their successful "transfer" into the new Romanian reality was usually facilitated by their financial and political status that they had built during the communist regime. Their "reinventing" of themselves was noticeable at mere street level, too. The first eye-catching shops in Kolozsvár, the city where I did my University studies, were opened by a lecturer in mathematics - a powerful, but dangerously incompetent, woman. Her husband had been a senior Party activist during the regime... He had not been powerful enough to be in the limelight, but he had amassed wealth and connections that allowed them to prosper in the new capitalist world.

Many thousands of such ghosts of the past were surfacing after the Revolution... Within just a few years, the circles of mid- and large-size businesses were closed; sometimes, some small enterprises could start up without many connections – but usually one had to be "in" with the new cliques.

It got to a point where an ordinary person could not even open a shop, without he or she paying off everybody; otherwise, one could not get building permits, or some puny health & safety inspection would have closed the business down. The "connected" people in the meantime easily built huge businesses, often completely illegally, without any building permits, tax returns, safety checks. A report by the Council of Europe's anti-money laundering committee stated that the "shadow economy" accounted for 28.4 percent of Romania's GDP in 2013. This means around 40 billion euros of uncollected taxes per year – a sum that is almost equal to amount of the entire tax revenue in Romania...

The outsiders, who could not operate in this shadow economy, were being drowned in endless bureaucracy; they were subjected to often-tragicomic voyages through the maze of mutually contradictory regulations.

One concrete example of the transformation of old crooks into new ones was offered in my hometown, where at one point a well-known criminal reinvented himself in the post-communist reality as the head of the local underworld. He was mainly preoccupied with the collection of protection money, and a bit of prostitution on the side - everyone should have a relaxing hobby. The chap was also organising break-ins into warehouses of imported goods... In his free time, he used to beat people up, whenever he took fancy to someone's girlfriend as he roamed the bars with his gorillas.

However, this was just "phase one" of the new Romanian evolutionary process...

In just a couple of years, he moved up to the level of major business circles in the city. He used to come to the riverside with his entire entourage during summer, bringing motorboats and water scooters, fooling around for hours up and down the river that was swarming with swimmers.

Then... he gradually vanished.

He disappeared from the news about shady events, which used to occur around him at street level. He, together with countless other such characters, elevated himself into the circles of real money and real power. He was still very active, with his entire so-called business network - but he no longer crossed the ordinary people's plane of existence. All such characters now operate cosily at the highest layers of the society...

The only law in that post-communist jungle capitalism was "acquire money by *any* means". This has not changed; people, who cannot experience the immense corruption in Romania on a daily basis, can read the EU and OCCRP reports... Laws and even paragraphs of the Constitution do not matter if they are obstacles to the interests of certain individuals or circles.

The mayor of my hometown disregarded and continues to disregard laws that protect the environment; he embarked on vast projects that massacred green areas, trees and natural habitats, in direct contradiction of applicable laws. He disregarded the laws and the sections of the Constitution, which state ethnic minority rights; he banned cultural festivals from the city, for several years refused to allow bilingual street signs. His various "business" interests and networks of connections protect him against most legal actions; nothing is more ironic than an utterly corrupt mayor loudly going on about anti-corruption measures.

Sometimes the perfectly innocent people can be mixed up in organised corruption, without even knowing it. Teachers in my hometown discovered that they were guarantors for a huge loan picked up by the school's director; she wanted to plug an increasingly gaping hole in her finances - she was running a huge loss-making business "on the side". The director had dived into the personnel files, used the personal details of a few teachers, and even forged their signatures on the loan application. Furthermore, she had also managed to pay off some people, who had "witnessed" the signing of the paperwork by the teachers... The whole matter came to light because the director was unable to pay back the loan, so the bank and the police began to chase the guarantors...

Now this is just one tiny example of fraud, but it shows what happens on those rare occasions when there is legal action taken against the perpetrators. Or rather, what does *not* happen; the culprit in this story was never punished, simply because her husband was very active in key political and so-called business circles... In contrast, some of the unwilling and unknowing guarantors were dragged through months of chaotic legal procedures, threats, insinuations, with the real risk of professional and financial ruin.

When a Hungarian ethnic mayor was elected in my hometown just after the Revolution, the joy of the Hungarian half of the city's population was quickly replaced by a realisation. We had a warm fuzzy feeling for a while, because our cultural identity had affirmed itself at the level of local administration. However, in the end it all came down to money; every political and administrative power in Bucharest boycotted him.

Funding was not approved for any of his projects, so not even the horrid pavements could be fixed. This was in a sheer contrast to his successor, the already mentioned ultra-corrupt Romanian mayor. Latter has had public funds pouring in from Bucharest. Funds allowed not just the re-paving of the entire city centre as a grand and visible gesture, but also paid for grand projects like that of a truly dazzling, albeit much needed, leisure resort on the riverside.

It reached a point where ethnic minority voters, who previously had always unconditionally asserted their ethnicity above all other considerations, began to consider the realities of the local administration… They began to put ethnic considerations aside and voted for this mayor in subsequent elections. As a further disillusionment, ethnic minority politicians, who had made a political career out of "raising their voice" for our basic rights, were making a fortune as they were exploiting their positions.

One local example was the *Hegyi Lajos Foundation*, which was freshly established in my high school in 1990, just after the Revolution. It was named after a maths teacher, who had been killed when the demonstrations, the about-to-become Revolution, had reached the streets of my hometown.

The foundation had been managed by the newly established RMDSZ, the Democratic Association of Hungarians in Romania; the annual prize, which was more than three times a good salary at that point in time, was awarded to high school graduates. The award was based on points calculated from achievements in a range of curricular and extra-curricular activities. It was a huge sum for an almost nineteen-year-old person. The double of this sum was to be awarded when the recipient finished studies at a Romanian University, and decided to remain in the country.

In the case of the first recipient of the award, the second stage never happened; the foundation's curator managed to make a cosy political career. Months were spent with chasing the elusive curator, just to find out whether the foundation's rules were still applicable. The curator eventually surfaced, saying that there was no money left. The whole foundation had gradually died of unnatural causes, while the curator established a profitable printing company... The foundation, with its laudable purpose of keeping talented youth in their home country, during the veritable exodus that occurred in early '90s, served a very different purpose... It had attracted funds from local and foreign donors, and then the funds were used for personal gains.

Once the foundation's managers had capitalised on this, there was no need for the Foundation, no need for the memory of who gave his name to it after he had given his life for the Revolution. Although the foundation continued for a while, it was eventually swallowed by the mud of corrupt egocentric manipulations. When latter were committed by ethnic minority politicians, there were huge rifts in their political organisations; the rifts were mainly between people who still had some moral backbone and the increasing majority, which lacked vital calcium in those bones...

A key figure of those years, one of the Messiahs of our newly regained ethnic identity, managed to obtain eight-figure sums in Hungarian forints for the funding, among other things, of the one and only youth magazine in Hungarian language. He became the new owner of that magazine, but a few months later, it was promptly discontinued by him, despite its huge success. He built a printing factory in the middle of nowhere, with dedicated water supply brought to it, wasting enormous sums of money.

It was not a surprise to find out that some of the new Hungarian ethnic minority politicians, who amassed considerable wealth in just a few years after the Revolution, had had close ties with the Securitate during Ceausescu's regime. No wonder that many Hungarians in Transylvania say nowadays that they can put up more easily with some of the corrupt Romanian politicians than with the corrupt Hungarian ones; the latter not only rob the country blind in the very same way, but at the same time they pretend that they are representing minority rights.

One can only hope that the new high society will clean up its act, that it will somehow ennoble itself over time.

People travel more, they see more, and now they can compare more. They have developed new needs. Yes, there are incredible kitsch villas being built, as the status symbols of this still primitive "elite" are large cars and villas – but tastes are gradually changing because needs are changing.

We can see new moguls, who wash their Lamborghini with buckets of soapy water; they do this not because they cannot afford a proper carwash, but because they are still eminently primitive people. Others build huge villas with truly monstrous architectural designs that are the laughing stock of the media; they keep rolled-up piles of handmade Persian rugs in bathtubs that they never use. Yes, many are still very primitive people, but they hold more power than any of the humble mortals could ever dream of.

The less tragicomic aspect is that the Hungarian minority has been used as pawn in the power games of both Romanian and Hungarian politicians. The RMDSZ has ruined its reputation by fraternising with any political party that was close to the positions of power.

The principal problem that the Hungarian minority is

suffering from is fragmentation at all levels, especially in Transylvania. This is nothing new; it, and the infighting it brought, has been a constant feature of Hungarian history. At present, too, whilst the public discourse is relentlessly emphasising the desperate need for a unified stance against the far right, the everyday reality is the opposite of that objective; on both small and large scale, Hungarians in Romania are split into myriad clusters of different opinions and attitudes.

On a microscopic scale, one can see this in various social media discussions that can lower themselves to kindergarten-level battles between opinions on how to "stick together". On a macroscopic scale, the same fragmentation and self-contradicting attitudes manifest themselves in the number of political parties and organisations that claim to be representing minority interests; however, they have been caught chasing their own agendas.

The resulting disillusionment has led to painful local and parliamentary election results for the Hungarian minority. In my hometown, the much despised ultra-corrupt city leadership has been voted into power several times, as most of the Hungarian minority voters (almost half of the city's voting population) could not see any point in taking part in the electoral process.

To make matters worse, even the most relevant and important political organisations, like the RMDSZ, have been seen opportunistically fraternising with just about any Romanian political force. The constant excuse voiced by RMDSZ politicians is that they try to be as close as possible to the power circles, so that they can better represent the Hungarian minority.

However, the factual reality is that any noteworthy achievement in terms of minority rights was the result of EU pressures and legislations, rather than their actual efforts. Furthermore, their opportunism, coupled with deplorable and visible fights for power within the RMDSZ, has regularly exhibited itself whenever they decided to ride waves stirred up by individuals or other small organisations. In such cases, the otherwise idling RMDSZ immediately steps forward with loud support for issues raised, and actively promoted, by others.

Electoral apathy is, of course, far from being a unique phenomenon in Eastern Europe or elsewhere for that matter. Nevertheless, the main problem for the Hungarian minority in Romania is that this apathy is in direct contradiction of what that minority needs. The inaction, opportunism, and fragmentation-producing power battles of Hungarian minority politicians led directly to this self-destructive apathy.

The Romanian political scene, as it has been between the two World Wars, belongs to short-term opportunists, who try to exploit their various positions of power during the short time periods that they manage to spent in those positions. They do this in a desperate hurry, because they know that the next bunch of crooks is just around the corner behind them, and they are aiming for the same seats.

Ultra-centralised power has always been the tradition in Romania. Naturally, before the Revolution this was quite obvious; however, even after nearly 25 years since the changes, any kind of decentralisation of power is still one of the major nightmares of Bucharest-based politicians. The recession actually heightened the tensions between the regions (or the "provinces" as Bucharest likes to call them) and the central government.

Regional administrative autonomy is an extremely sensitive subject in Romania, especially when Transylvania is bringing it up. Such autonomy-related discussions trigger all the possible anti-Hungarian rhetoric, and all the possible paranoia about Transylvania as a territory. However, quite ironically, many Transylvanian-born Romanians (not the ones moved there by Ceausescu) are supporting the idea; the similarity with the Catalan situation's central issues is very strong.

Transylvania, after all, is an economic powerhouse; the GDP per capita is around 10% higher than the Romanian average. However, as in the Catalan case, money is vanishing toward Bucharest – the tensions that this fact has been increasingly causing have been greatly heightened by the recent economic recession. Thus, there is more and more concrete discourse about various shades of autonomy, but politicians in Bucharest, together with the ultra-nationalist mass media, are always throwing major tantrums about the mere mentioning of the topic.

Intentionally, administrative and territorial autonomy is confused, and many Romanians, who simply lack the even basic understanding of the difference between the two, or of the facts that the discussions are based on, are jumping on the anti-Hungarian bandwagon. Time will tell, whether some sanity will be gradually infused into these discussions. However, the fact that the topic makes Romanian politicians immediately pull out the ethnic card, hence completely divert attention from the core issues, is not a promising sign.

Ethnic tensions always won votes for them after the Revolution, and this will continue; the matter of Transylvanian autonomy of any kind will not be possible to discuss lucidly in Romania for quite some time…

XVII. MONEY

Corruption has soared to heights that were previously unimaginable, taking over all the layers of our society. It was a result of a number of factors, but the typical Balkan mentality and the unstoppable diminishing of the buying power of the new Romanian currency played a central role. As one looked at how corruption is used by those in power, there is the other side of the coin, too - money itself, as end goal of petty or high-level corrupt practices.

During communism, a box of proper chocolate or a small bag of real coffee had been enough to make some crucial paper pusher do the paper pushing, but after the Revolution, the value of expected, or even demanded, bribes started to go up. Bribes were needed for jobs, too in the most sought-after areas like banking and telecoms, which have been paying handsome salaries. Some of my colleagues, after they had finished University, would have had to pay huge bribes for such jobs unless they were well connected; these bribes were quite paradoxical: if one could pay such sums, then one really did not need such a job... Many such bribes were no longer expressed in the local currency, because of the skyrocketing inflation; they recipients demanded hard currency, dollars or, later on, euros.

The country, which essentially had misinterpreted freedom as a state in which anybody can do *anything*, became the stage for surreal drama. If you had money, and connections that dated back to the times of the former regime, you really could do anything.

The absorption of EU development funds has been extremely low, as highlighted repeatedly by puzzled EU officials. One often wonders how there can be so much puzzlement, because the explanation is visible every day in Romania - and it is a remarkably simple one... One would actually expect EU development funds to be absorbed very rapidly, and then, of course, misdirected by corrupt schemes inside Romania.

However, reality is much simpler. Essentially, the circles that generate enormous profits with extremely lucrative and self-sustaining corrupt schemes simply do not bother to go through the various application phases, nor the detailed and large amount of paperwork needed for obtaining slices of those funds. Many smaller, honest businesses have been applying, but the corrupt "big fish" do not need such tedium to pocket the same (or much larger) amounts of money.

Many EU regulations have been turned into moneymaking schemes. In the great Romanian tradition, façade is everything - and, once again, the simple everyday issues provide the best examples of what lies behind the façade. For instance, special recycling bins had been imported, only later manufactured, and deployed - without the actual infrastructure having existed for recycling; the handling, transport and, of course, the processing of the to-be-recycled waste is still missing in many places.

The perfect symbol for this was a three-in-one recycling bin I saw on my hometown's riverside promenade; it had just one black bin bag under its plastic cover that had three different holes for plastic, paper and glass. The environmentalist facade is very useful for justifying the various (and vast) sums diverted to environmental matters, while officials were indiscriminately destroying green areas, building businesses with immeasurable environmental footprints, or setting up areas where wealthy foreigners could hunt protected species of animals. Some of the latter are actually bred at specialised "farms"; an acquaintance of mine, who was fortunate to get a very lucrative contract for installing electrical fences around these above-and-behind-the-law "businesses", was shocked to realise the size of this extremely profitable part of the Romanian tourism industry...

However, there have been countless "ordinary" cases of corruption, too – especially before the country joined the EU. Senators had been landing entire airplane loads of smuggled cigarettes, and made billions in local currency from such illegal imports. Other members of the Parliament had had, metaphorically speaking, seemingly endless convoys of illegally imported cars coming into the country. Still, such news and facts that used to come to light were soon eclipsed by stories of true *tours de force* in post-communist moneymaking.

One key political figure of the '90s, together with one of the still key Hungarian minority politicians from Transylvania, began to cut the forests on the two sides of the Carpathian Mountains – they sold vast amounts of timber, and, naturally, everything was done illegally. This had hit the pages of certain brave newspapers, but factual mass media articles had never led to the resignation or the punishment of politicians of such stature. Furthermore, the public thought that it was, and still is, *expected* of such people to be entirely corrupt; a factual confirmation of the latter did not surprise people.

The key figure of RMDSZ (the Democratic Association of Hungarians in Romania), who was responsible for the vast illegal deforestation in three counties, was nicknamed God's Chainsaw. The biggest problem is not that this still powerful "businessman" and politician has amassed enormous wealth at the expense of unprecedented areas of ancient forests. The critical issue is that this very deforestation was the main cause of devastating flash floods that rushed down from the mountains several times, and virtually removed from the face of the Earth a number of settlements. Someone with this track record is still at the forefront of political life, and he is pretty much dictating how businesses are run in those three counties. The similarities between this character and a Mafia *Don* were and are just too obvious not to be made in the media and in the public's mind.

It was also quite amusing, that when greed operated on a national scale and/or at the level of the Parliament and Government, then ethnic aspects did not matter. The new "businessmen" of any ethnicity collaborated in perfect harmony, without the usual and difficult ethnic tensions.

However, as it happened in the case of the aforementioned God's Chainsaw, if there is any revelation about the minority Mafiosi, or any even fact-based criticism aimed at them, then these Hungarian and other minority characters play the role of martyrs. Simply put, they are the first ones to point out that they are merely the victims of attacks by Romanian nationalists...

One brilliant example of utter corruption, topped by total hypocrisy, was that the same Hungarian minority politician, who had cut and sold our forests illegally, lectured schoolteachers on strike. The strike was about the abysmal salaries that could not even cover the energy bills, but this multi-billionaire senator preached to these teachers about the fact that everybody should have had two jobs in Romania, in order to cope with the economic realities. The outrage was unfortunately only limited to some phone calls to that radio station. On one hand, nobody was shocked nor surprised by saintly, preaching Mafiosi with attitude; on the other hand, many still lacked the courage to criticise the ruling classes – old fears had not gone away easily.

Another such Hungarian minority moral beacon was lecturing the country's youth about not leaving the country. An obvious question was how could such a person, who had made hundreds of millions in local currency in a time span of just six years, have the audacity to lecture poor students who could see their future only in the promising West? It is not difficult to imagine why the continual contradiction between the apparent moral stance taken by some key public figures and their perceived (or factual) corruption managed to enrage ordinary people.

Even in the South of the country, not just in Transylvania, many high school pupils and university students can barely wait to finish their studies and leave the country. They simply cannot see a decent future for themselves – the grey matter "export" has not slowed down since the Revolution, instead it gathered pace. One of my friend's wife has her calendar filled by language lessons she holds for students, who want to learn more German and English, because their plan is to go abroad as soon as they get their diplomas.

It was hard for us to keep track of the leading politicians, because everybody in Government used to spend only a few months in their seats; they quickly filled their bank accounts, and then they were replaced by others. One transport minister, questioned on one of the national news channels, could not say what the price of an underground ticket was in Bucharest. They were and are completely out of touch even with their own area of responsibility, let alone the everyday realities of the electorate.

A finance minister was given a wad of cash, on national TV; it represented the measly average income at that time, and he was asked to give an example of how would a person use that money to pay average bills, to buy average amount of food, and so on. He was unable even to begin the calculations. Those layers of the new political powers were, and still are, completely out of touch with reality; they are all locked within the virtual walls of their separate Universe, only being preoccupied with stealing as much as they can while they are in power.

The art and the science of corruption were brought to a level never seen even during the communist regime; a completely new breed of high-powered "businessmen" were surfacing and shaping our new reality. It was not just the good old Romanian who-knows-who system, but also the who-does-what-for-whom-in-return-for-what system. As a philosophical taxi driver told me once, the main difference between the USA and Romania is that the USA is the land where everything is possible, while Romania is the land where *anything* is possible...

When Romania geared up to join the EU, suddenly a whole range of anti-corruption agencies and organisations were set up, as a nicely painted façade for the West to see; National Anti-Corruption Division. National Integrity Agency – all very nice names. One could phone in even, and could report corruption via a freephone number. The fight was on... or so it seemed on the surface. No sane ordinary person would have dared to phone in about some "witnessed" corruption, giving full personal details. Even the police is owned by the underworld; even lesser crooks, for example a petty fraudster who is a youth water polo coach in the city, who had stolen from sponsors, parents and the kids, and was sacked already by two sport clubs, are actually employed by the local police force... It is a perfect symbol of current Romanian realities, when this very fraudster is threatening to unleash his colleagues on a sponsor whom he had stolen from...

A woman, who was in charge of a major private investment fund, quietly drove one day to the airport, and vanished with an eight-figure sum in dollars. Interpol spent years searching for her – then, one day, she turned up at the Otopeni international airport in Bucharest. She said that she had sort-of "woken up" in Greece, and that she had vaguely remembered where she was from. She had no recollection of her fraud, well, no memory of anything. During the tragicomic and corrupt courtroom battle that followed, she was acquitted because of total amnesia... Then she left the country again, on the first flight out of there.

However, these were just a few scandals of the Romanian '90s and noughties, which exploded around high-profile public figures... The stories around more faceless individuals were sometimes equally, if not more, surreal. The Italian mafia should have come to Romania to re-train in truly new and inspired ways of making money. Actually, Interpol caught several key figures of the Camorra, who had been living in Romania for several years; they had installed themselves very neatly, and had been arranging their "affairs" from Romania.

As there was no real limit to this tragicomedy, some much publicised cases of corruption and fraud indeed surreal.

A company, with good connections, was contracted to resurface many roads in the Moldova region of the country. They must have forgotten to pay somebody off, otherwise we never would have found out about the story. They, in a way that proved the general theory of relativity via a genuinely Romanian experiment, shifted kilometre stones along major roads to a distance of around 900 meters from each other. They walked away with 10% of the materials and money. However, one morning, an old man noticed a kilometre stone in an odd place in his native village... Within days, the entertaining story was in the papers, the scheme was discovered, but no heads rolled...

Only corruption and greed were progressing rapidly in the Romania of the 1990s... As the 2013 EU report on corruption, plus the OCCRP's top "prize" for the most corrupt European country shows, it still remains the only thing that really works smoothly in that country.

Disease is huge business, but whilst major pharmaceutical companies are investigated for bribe and price fixing in the West and Far East, Romanian companies that distribute pharma goods have never been investigated. The most recent in-your-face corrupt deal was the one related to the distribution of antivirals, when the novel flu epidemics caused global panic. The tender for the contract specified requirements in ludicrous level of detail, including the exact number of warehouses and vans per county that the winning company had to have. However, the real sign of corruption, promptly denied by the Government, was that only one company in the country "happened" to have the exactly matching features and facilities... It is a classic method of awarding contracts in other countries, too, but in Romania this is done very openly as there are no real consequences.

The former mayor of Kolozsvár (or Cluj) lifted anti-minority chauvinism and corruption to stratospheric heights; I had the dubious pleasure of doing my University studies exactly during his regime. The pyramid scheme run by his entourage was called, ironically, *Caritas*. It had collected immense sums of money from people... It initially did pay out the promised 800% returns after a three-month period; this was the bait - hence, many began to deposit various sums of money that ranged from some savings to *all* savings.

In some cases, huge loans were secured on the family homes of people, who were floating on the clouds of their truly naive dreams of quasi-instantaneous wealth... The wave of initial payouts kept the marketing machine going, and it convinced people about the potential of the scheme. Countless families travelled there from distant villages and cities. It functioned for a short while, and then, inevitably, the pyramid scheme collapsed. By then, apart from a number of fortunate early clients who received their payments, the organisers of the scheme had managed to get their hands on vast sums of money.

After the collapse *Caritas*, its real key figures have never been prosecuted, except for a few scapegoats. Within a few months after the collapse, organised circles, which had been directly linked to *Caritas*, began to invest in vast new building projects, businesses, countless small and private banks – and everything in that city began to grow like mushrooms during a wet autumn... but it was raining with *Caritas* money.

The mayor of that city made even Ceausescu look like an amateur when it came to greed; his downright pathological obsessions re-shaped the city. While there was no money for basic things, like road repairs, the mayor was erecting statues after statues.

Some of these statues managed to dwarf even the city's opera house. The costs of the new statues, which were made with criminally bad taste by astonishingly terrible "artists", could have paved all the roads of the county. He had set himself the aim of making sure that everybody in the city, every minute of every day, would be forever reminded about what country the city belongs to. In order to establish sure signs that revisionist Hungarian tanks have not invaded the city, the paranoid mayor ordered the placing of Romanian flags on every single lamppost and public building in the city...

Furthermore, he ordered the painting of *every* bench and garbage bin with the colours of the Romanian flag... This was not nationalism; this was a psychiatric condition that was using up vast public funds. On those benches, the contractors had made a hilarious mistake: they had painted the colours of the flag in reverse order... Hence, everything was re-painted. Whatever the cost was, at least the ordinary people of the city, who used to break their ankles in the potholes of the dismally lit streets, could see national flags and tricolour garbage bins everywhere...

Having been obsessed by the glorious Dacian continuity theory of professor Daicoviciu, this local ruler instructed unqualified workers to dig everywhere, especially near monuments of a Hungarian past. A beautiful piazza, which surrounded the gothic St. Michael cathedral and was a true gem of the city centre, was virtually ruined by barbarous, so-called archaeological, digging. Even the decent and sane Romanian population complained about it, and forgot the manipulated ethnic tensions between them and the Hungarian minority.

The excavations were eventually abandoned; the workers left behind piles of dug up soil, which later spread as mud onto the surrounding streets. During the dry weeks of the hot summer, winds carried it further as dust, and then rain turned it again into a thin layer of yellowish mud. This, as many of the mayor's other demented schemes, was successful in vandalising not just the monuments he sought to destroy, but also the everyday look of the city.

The Hungarian and Latin inscriptions on the magnificent group of statues in the same piazza, statues that were immortalising king Mathias Corvinus, had been brutally knocked down one night - and were replaced with a Romanian inscription about a Romanian king.

Things have improved; he is no longer in power. Even the benches and garbage bins were repainted with normal colours.

That long period that the city spent under him is still perhaps the brightest example of just how the country functioned even after radical changes... It still is an amalgam of localised concentrations of vast wealth and corrupt networks, which connect all layers of the society. It is a country of maximally exploited ultra-nationalism, of complete disregard for laws and the Constitution, of buried, but continuously over-compensated, historical guilt, of an utter denial of the past...

An almost exact copy of that former mayor is the current mayor of my hometown. He, with his entourage, has been in power for more than a decade. People have voted for him repeatedly, as he knew exactly whom he was dealing with – and he always perfectly exploited the various interests, tensions, even ethnic minority issues in the city.

He is another totalitarian ruler, albeit a local one. He regularly disregards the Constitution, the laws; he acts in direct opposition of those whenever it comes to his financial or political interests. He is, exactly as the mayor of Cluj was, allergic to the city's historic landmarks and unique personality. From the barbarous destruction of decorative trees from main promenades to the reshaping of the historic city centre, from the illegal ban on certain Hungarian minority festivals to the contracts handed out to companies owned by his family and clique, he certainly had made his mark on that city.

Such public figures have eloquently shown that there is and, for quite some time, there will be no real consequences of certain deeds... The newspapers can publish anything on colossal frauds committed by senators, mayors, MPs – but usually only the small fish get caught in the net of the various anti-corruption agencies.

The clergy, especially the scandalous upper echelons of the Romanian Orthodox Church that have been widely and rightly attacked in the more lucid press, is also an embodiment of greed and of the "anything is possible" Romanian ethos. Apart from the vast state funds that they receive in exchange for vital services performed during election campaigns, or the exorbitant sums they demand for religious services performed at weddings and such events, they run private businesses, too. An infamous Orthodox priest, who drives around in a red Porsche, has been running a national network of sex shops – in a slight contrast with the medieval ultra-prudish nonsense he preaches.

In order to show to the EU that Romania is genuinely fighting corruption, despite the OCCRP report on how even the Romanian Parliament continuously and actively facilitates corruption with its often-surreal "legislation", there are many show trials. In the great Stalinist tradition, the big fish bring the old, no longer useful, or small fish to trial. Whilst my hometown's mayor could not account for a sum of 3.2 million in Romanian new currency (RON), he was sending a swimming pool administrator's file to the anti-corruption agency. That administrator was accused of stealing some thousands of Euros…

Often such local cases offer the best symbolic examples of the entire Romanian *modus operandi*. The aforementioned swimming pool was turned into a covered one by the mayor, during one of his election campaigns; this transformation triggered a superb renaissance in my hometown, which has always been known for the swimming and water polo talents it nurtured, and even exported, in the past. Unfortunately, since the Revolution, water polo virtually had been hibernating in lack of training facilities – until this 50-metre pool was covered and hence made usable in the autumn-to-spring period, too.

However, as soon as the mayor was re-elected, he began to complain about the losses the pool was making, the operational costs and so on. He has been constantly threatening with the closure of the pool, or at least the removal of the tent that is covering it. The threats so far could not be transformed into reality, as there are more than seven hundred children training there – and many have influential parents.

Nobody, not even the so-called journalists who have been repeating the mayor's aberrations like some parrots, posed the rhetorical question: how do profits, operational costs and losses even come into the discussion about a pool made and sustained from public funds? Nobody asks about the vast income that the leisure resort around the pool generates each year, or about the fact that sport actually has good funding in the city. Correction: certain sports, simply because of personal interests and fraud activities milking the public funds, are allocated vast sums of money, even if they produce zero results.

An example is football, where the deputy mayor has special "interests"; the city's football team is playing in a low-life league, but they are allocated such funds from public money, that they even go to "training matches" in Kuwait for example, and they stay in the most luxurious hotels. In contrast, numerous swimmers have won gold and many other medals at national and even international competitions, the water polo girls have been national champions several times – but water sports that continue to produce superb results are allocated infinitesimal funds by the mayor.

If one zooms in, the small space around that swimming pool is heaving with several swim and water polo clubs. They constantly fight each other for strange definitions of "power", fame and money. The fact that certain characters there are proven fraudsters is a small matter in the grand scheme of things - so is the fact that they are allowed to get anywhere near children… However, perhaps more importantly, one can see club presidents chase personal gain via any means – even by torpedoing the city's reputation, its financial wellbeing and last, but not least, its athletes.

One such local president recently held on to his seat in the country's water polo Federation by playing into the hands of the shady characters in the Federation's remaining leadership committee. His tactics included even the sabotage of a national children's championship that would have been organised in my hometown – but, in order to exploit tensions between clubs and between the North and South clans of the Federation, he lied that the pool would not have had any water in it due to maintenance works. It is a mere irony that his own club's players at the same time were given special permissions by the mayor's office to continue training in the pool, whilst staff was on holiday for a few weeks…

The same president could even play into the hands of the same Federation characters, when latter wanted to remove from the list of already officially qualified teams a few Transylvanian teams, so that Bucharest in the so-called South zone of the national championships could have had more teams. Thus, a president of a junior sport club in my hometown, apparently working on the resurrection of a once superbly successful sport in the city, can torpedo the very city and the very sport he has the duty to nurture. The children and their sport do not matter in the machinations for dubious power.

Greed is present in other sport federations, too; two characters from the Romanian Cycling Federation have been in the crosshairs of the police, because they defrauded nearly half a million in local currency. In a truly Balkan way, they turned up eventually at a police station with a bag of money, in the hope that their sentence will be more lenient. It would have been slightly more stylish to use a briefcase instead of a bag…

XVIII. EXCHANGE

We exchanged a world of constant terror for a relatively free one. To many people, the former oppressed world had meant stable jobs and guaranteed housing. That world had had a fictitious economy, in which salaries and pensions had been able to cover the costs of a very modest and predictable, perhaps too predictable, existence. It had been an unimaginably monotonous and constrained existence - but to many, that very monotony had actually meant stability.

Therefore, just a few years after the Revolution, many people have been feeling a strange, often inexplicable, nostalgia for the totalitarian regime. The West, and some of us, has been watching that nostalgia with quite some surprise. Western media was surprised whenever some ex-communist country, just a few years after the changes, voted for faces from its dark past. It was always the result of nostalgia for regimes, whose memory gradually softened in people's minds. People, after the social and political paradigm shifts, were suddenly assaulted by unfamiliar feelings and states of mind: worries about jobs, surreal inflation, heating bills, omnipresent corruption, and millions of other new uncertainties.

Before the collapse of Ceausescu's stage props that had lasted for decades, people, self- or at least semi-consciously, had been using various methods of escapism to soften the system's assaults on their minds... Therefore, after the Revolution that had safely demolished those stage props, people in vast numbers began to avert their gaze from the terrestrial, unrecognisable, and chaotic reality that was unfolding around them – they began to look toward the heavens...

This was not simply a new tidal wave of interest in religion, the occult, or science fiction. It was an almost pathological obsession with paranormal phenomena, the occult, UFOs, collective delusions... Innumerable such articles, magazines, seminars, clubs, and societies turned up in a matter of a few months. By the summer of 1990, vast numbers of people were diving into the new pool of sometimes valid, but most of the times wildly aberrant studies, articles, talks, presentations, and pseudo-documentaries on these subjects.

Such topics were equally accessible and were open for debate before the Revolution. Still, it was at the beginning of the '90s, when there was a sudden explosion of interest in, and very often obsession with, these subjects. Only after the Revolution did so many crop circles turn up on the fields of Romania. Only then did UFOs in great numbers decide to travel across the gulfs of space to watch us in our post-Revolutionary state of stupor. UFO sightings were being reported on a weekly basis in 1990...

People ventured into dark forests and climbed mountains in order to observe the visitors from outer space. Ghosts, too, which for some reason had been dormant during the communist decades, turned up in great numbers, and started to haunt various old buildings...

I still doubt that all this was just a coincidence. There was no political factor, which could have explained why all of this only happened after the radical changes. Furthermore, we all witnessed a gradual return to normality after a just a few years: most of these clubs, magazines, and even entire subject areas sunk to appropriate levels of (in) significance in daily life.

I think that the entire phenomenon was one of the many manifestations of a "post-traumatic stress syndrome" experienced at a national scale, in the Romania of the early 1990s.

There are theories about why the number of UFO sightings had spiked in the USA always in strict correlation with major social and/or political changes. Were these an expression of the collective psyche, desperately looking for "meaning"? Traditional belief systems had been similarly replaced with the obsession with the paranormal and the occult in many people's minds in the Romanian '90s, too. A desperate need for clear signs, directions, and guidance was projected into another sphere.

Since the reality wrapped around people's fragile and new everyday life did not provide answers, people were trying to find answers "out there". Others were seeking answers inside them, they were seeking secret and miraculous mental powers to cope... hence some new psychobabble was the answer.

The people, who flooded the cities with countless seminars about subjects like self-help, positive thinking and so on, were tapping into the same psychological needs that the UFO and paranormal "experts" were. Both the outer and inner space gave countless *promises* of answers to the vast numbers of people.

I have known several people, who went from one seminar to the other, from one belief system to countless others, seeking themselves, wanting so desperately to believe in something that gives them some inner peace that they did not care what it is as long as it "works". Scientology and other such exploitative, often downright dangerous, "religions" have turned this to their advantage. One of my friends had become a fervent scientologist, tried to convert us – and eventually vanished. Apparently, he was taken to the USA by the "church", but his parents and everyone else have completely lost contact with him. Perhaps he is happier now... depending on how one defines happiness.

Kids could see their parents working extremely hard, trying to have a minimally decent life in the new world, a world in which street signs that wore then names of old communist "heroes" had barely been replaced. The promises, according to which the painful "transition phase" (to borrow Ion Iliescu, the neo-communist first leader's term) was to be a short one, kept coming... Years had gone by, while things got more and more difficult for those who wanted to be able to afford at least the everyday basics.

Freedom of thought and expression had come at a price. When a teacher friend of mine asked the pupils about their favourite literary characters, she was quite stunned by the answers that she received in the mid-1990s. The evil characters, who double-crossed everybody in the great romantic novels, had become role models because "they were ambitious", as the kids put it.

However, by the late 1990s, kids concluded that having an aim in life was nonsense, as one would only suffer disappointment. In their minds, it was pointless to study, because parents with diplomas could barely pay the utility bills... It was pointless to work so hard, put in overtime, or even have two jobs, because people could barely afford the everyday basics.

Poverty became widespread. I doubt that there are many countries in the EU, where fast food chains employ people tasked with keeping beggars away from the terraces and tables... Security guards in train stations like the *Gara de Nord* in Bucharest are still trying to keep the shady characters away from the waiting rooms, platforms and snack bars... Street kids, organised into gangs, offer to carry your luggage, descending upon you like very hungry hawks... and they have a sixth sense for spotting people with money, no matter how plainly one dresses for travel.

It was not surprising that, according to statistics, the average people in the new Romania were spending almost 90% of their income on bills and food. The society became completely polarised, only two opposites existed, with not much in-between: a thin froth of the extremely rich and thick sediment of the poor. So, kids could conclude: there was no point in aiming for a life with qualifications, since they would not be able to get a decent job if they stayed in Romania.

Is it not ironic that the more misery there is the more prize draws one sees on TV? It was very difficult to find adverts in the new Romania that did not state one's chance of winning some shiny prize, anything from a car to huge sums of money, even a house sometimes...

Even the huge debate around Romania's joining of NATO produced enormous profit for the private TV channel ProTV. For many months, people kept sending in "votes" on postcards sold at 30 times the price of a normal postcard - and posted them to the TV station's address. The vote had absolutely no connection with, nor effect on, the real factors weighed by NATO officials. The vast majority of marketing tricks in Romania are still based on the promise of prizes; people worship the fuzzy silhouette of mathematically improbable fortune...

Theatres, cinemas, concert halls, orchestras, well, anything cultural, have also been exposed to the new economy. Stable and sufficient state funding was just a distant memory. Ironically, the communist state's funding had been vastly more beneficial compared to that of the jungle capitalism, which burst through the cracks of the terminally aged pavements of the new Romania. Libraries had been able to fill their shelves with books bought from state funds... Theatre companies and orchestras had been able to focus on the content; after the changes, they had to focus on the number of sold tickets...

Theatres slid into a desperate form of commercialism, with naked actors running around the stage in "new" versions of some plays. Concerts were featuring a veritable salad of movie tunes, mixed with fragmented "chart" classics.

Bookshops, like everything meant to feed the mind and soul, have begun to shrink; many have disappeared. The very few surviving, struggling bookstores are selling expensive books; books have become a luxury...

Local film festivals, too were struggling every year to find sponsors, despite their steadily growing success, the increasing quality of submitted works, and the growing interest from the public... Good quality magazines struggled for survival, despite the number of readers - many disappeared purely because of re-prioritisation of funding.

For a while, Hungarian minority press and art, emerging from decades of oppression, has been treated with a rather unhealthy reverence by the same minority. If something was Hungarian, then it was automatically something of great quality; any criticism of the output of local Hungarian authors and artists caused outrage. The usual defence one could hear was that one should be happy that these works exist, and they are "ours". Thankfully, "ours", as a qualitative category and as an automatic seal of approval, has gradually faded as years went by. With the increase in the output of Hungarian minority authors, and the connections built by them with the media and art communities in Hungary and other countries, there was gradually a more balanced and certainly more selective judgment of minority works.

However, at the start of the 1990s, people were buying "must have" items like mobile phones; they were replacing their rusty, disintegrating, communist-era cars with extraordinarily expensive new ones. They paid back the loans that had huge interest rates due to high inflation in the 1990s; they somehow managed to pay the bills... and they had no money left for culture and arts. Therefore, a commercialisation of the cultural scene, combined with the financial situation of the majority of the population, led to the characteristic post-communist (anti-)cultural phenomenon witnessed in Romania, too.

Moral survival, and abstract concepts like freedom of speech, plummeted on the priority list of the ordinary people. Such "luxuries" paled in significance, when compared to the struggles for everyday basics.

Unfortunately, one of my friends became an example of how extreme people's reactions could become to a never before experienced, seemingly unpredictable world that they were not equipped to cope with. He changed into a deeply paranoid individual after the Revolution; his reaction to life's myriad new uncertainties was to become suspicious of everything and everybody... Ironically, this mental shift occurred just when one no longer had to be careful about one's expressed thoughts.

He had developed a complete system of delusions. At first, the freemasons had been hunting for him because of his "revelatory" programmes. Then an obsession with UFOs and extra-terrestrials followed. Later, his paranoid delusions focused again on more earthly things, as he dived headfirst into an ocean of paranormal mumbo-jumbo to protect himself against dark forces.

He re-arranged his flat into "energy zones", and used to place strange concoctions on the floor; these made me fall over, whenever I was trying to get in and out of his living room that was filled with his vast music collection. Those odd concoctions were meant to protect him from negative energies...

After the demise of institutionalised terror, paranoia was no longer an effective survival mechanism. Some minds just folded over, curled up, and began to see threats in everything, as the former constant daily routines had changed to a new chaos. There was order in my friend's paranoia, in his imagined dangers - an order, which his mind desperately needed, while it was trying to deal with a total reality shift around him.

It all may sound overblown for someone who lives comfortably in a well-established economic and political system. However, the post-Revolution Romania was a place of radical change, a country where people had to realise: they were not prepared for the aftermath of the 1989 big bang; an utterly alien reality was being unleashed around them.

Still, to this day, they are in the process of switching from a Kafkaesque to a Borgesian nightmare, in which they are trying to find their way out of a labyrinth with no centre...

XIX. EXPERIMENT

The first five years that followed the 1989 Revolution were mostly marked by my University studies. The entire education system was changing, and it was basically experimenting on us, the first generation of post-Revolution students. Some things remained unchanged, for example the weekly 38-40 hours of courses, lab sessions, and countless seminars.

I was studying in Kolozsvár (Cluj in Romanian language, a historic Transylvanian city only hundred-odd kilometres away from my hometown. We used to call the process of getting to University and back windsurfing. The reason for the name was that we used to ride on completely packed buses; due to the horrid public transport system of that large city, these buses were rare occurrences. So, the many hundreds of students travelling between the lecture halls and the residence halls most often ended up holding on to the vertical bars in the middle of the buses' doorways. We used to stand on the edge of the bus that travelled with its doors open. Today's health and safety bureaucrats would have had a very unhealthy and unsafe heart attack, if they saw this. With our faces in the wind, with us leaning outward, pushed out by the amalgam of bodies that was bulging from these metal boxes on wheels, we looked like windsurfers... and it used to fun in -20 degrees centigrade during winter...

Exactly as it did during the years of the communist energy saving measures, the free Romania continued to apply absurd principles when it came to something as basic as heating. The residence halls used to be ice cold during the winter, so we spent the nights in sleeping bags covered with the duvets, and we wore woolly hats. The rooms could get so cold during the winter that water often froze in the glasses left near the window.

In spring, the new fuel quotas used to be set for the heating centres. The latter, as they always did in the previous decades, were burning all the fuel that was left over after winter, due to idiotic (and no longer ideological) energy saving measures. During March and April, our windows and doors were kept constantly open to create some extra ventilation; even so, many of us had to escape downtown from the overheated rooms...

What made these oven-like residence halls even more ironic during those spring months was that the administrators often had to resort to draconian measures to control the use of electrical heaters during winter. They even tried to confiscate the heaters we used to bring with us, because the buildings' wiring simply could not handle the load.

The normal fuses would have melted, as each of the thirty-odd rooms on each floor had one or two kilowatts eaten up by often-improvised heaters; thus, we had to be inventive. In the boys' residence halls, 60mm nails were employed instead of fuses; the girls used several hairpins... The smell of the burning plastic insulation, as the wires in the walls were heating up, used to be a sure sign of imminent electrical meltdown.

I used to live on the ground floor, where the main distribution panel was hiding in a small, always unlocked room – it was the holy shrine of electricity... This shrine was our only for some elements of end-of-20th century existence: light and civilised temperatures in our rooms...

Whenever the shrine burned down, it took the technicians a couple of weeks to replace the entire thing. The administrators had a stable routine - no punishments, just firm threats of confiscating all electrical heaters and radiators. Considering how much we were taking the entire electrical system outside its specifications, it managed to take quite admirable amounts of desperate abuse from the students.

A few times, while the wiring was preparing itself for its usual fiery death, the voltage dropped so much due to the terminal overload that the light bulbs' filaments were glowing faintly, like pale red spirals. The very old valve TV sets, with their ancient voltage regulators, were the funniest during these pre-meltdown periods. The black-and-white TV sets soldiered on, or at least tried to; they used to paint a smaller and smaller, fainter and fainter picture on the screen, and eventually the picture was reduced to a palm-sized grey blob in the middle of the screen. At that point, we usually gave up watching the psychedelic TV show, which was a result of our criminally improvised, but desperate, heating solutions...

The administrators never changed their heating policies; possibly, they were subject to higher-up ex-communist regulations; so the technicians kept rewiring the whole blooming thing, cursing and abusing the students. We knew that no serious retaliation was possible, as we would have seriously kicked their heads in; nobody needed in those days and years student riots and possibly clashes with police commandos... as some that did happen in Bucharest were feeding the international media.

Our central heating regime brought just a few hours of lukewarm water into our radiators each day. Somewhere, in somebody's newly liberated post-Revolutionary skull, replacing burnt fuse panels and miles of wiring several times during winter was cheaper, than proper central heating given to us, the "future of new Romania".

The enthusiastic and eager-to-learn students used to arrive every autumn to conquer rooms in those soon-to become-caves-of-ice residence halls. Yes, *conquer* - as I cannot find any other word for the process that was needed to obtain a room with three, then later, as overcrowding took hold, with six or seven roommates... There were no lists, no assigned rooms and beds, just a designated day of accommodation hell.

I used to travel up to Kolozsvár at dawn, and then queued up before sunrise. By the time the Sun paid us a visit, we were a compact mass of young, shivering human bodies pressed together, waiting for the administrator in front of some residence hall. When he finally made an appearance, the crowd, more exactly the first couple of hundred luckier students, pushed their way in, and went up the stairs to the first floor - where the God of Rooms had been preparing to wield his ballpoint pen.

We used to be reduced to an animalistic state; the crowd was so desperate and tightly compressed, that those in the middle of it used to ask those at the edges to tell them what time it was. We were not even able to free our arms sufficiently to check the time, or to eat something...

I used to have a small water bottle in one coat pocket, a sandwich and some chocolate in the other. If we managed to end up inside the building, and got close to the administrators' all-powerful ballpoint pen, then we had a real chance of getting a room. Others often had to come back the next day, and eventually the limited number of rooms ran out – so the rest of the students had to consider privately rented accommodation in the city. Latter was, by an order of magnitude, more expensive...

Getting a key early on, among the first few hundred students, had advantages - we could immediately begin to scavenge in the building. Since many rooms had been looted during the summer holidays, often even basic furniture was missing – so we had to gather shelves, beds, tables, and chairs from whatever rooms with broken locks we could find those in. We used to combine all the elements into a rudimentary, but functional, arrangement. Then, during the following autumn, the whole tragicomedy repeated itself...

The number of students kept going up and up, but the number of available residence halls stayed the same... Therefore, by the time we were in our fifth, and final, year of studies, we had developed our routine of bribing the administrative machinery. This meant that we could get our room back the following autumn, and never have extra people crammed into it.

The rooms were getting crowded, many ended up accommodating seven or eight people. Depending on the weather, the students used to escape to libraries, parks, or just onto the flat rooftops of the residence halls, so that they could concentrate. It was simply impossible to co-exist in such crowded rooms...

In terms of heating and conditions to study in, the lecture theatres, laboratories and seminar rooms were not any better. After the Revolution, Universities did not receive proper funding. Thus, rudimentary equipment and ancient instruments were our main tools in the labs.

In lecture theatres, the main tools of our learning were not the pens and notebooks, but the thickest jumpers and socks we could wear... We used to sit for six, sometimes eight, hours a day in the literally freezing lecture halls of the new Romania, in which heated classrooms were still considered a luxury.

A line from one of Neil Simon's plays was perfectly applicable to those winters: the radiators were the coldest objects in our rooms... I used to enjoy the power electronics laboratories, because there we could measure things like the short circuit currents of large electrical motors... Thus, in a laboratory with just six degrees Celsius, I could take my gloves off and I could warm my hands above the buzzing, overheating coils of some large motor.

Then, in spring, exactly as our residence hall rooms did, the lecture and lab rooms used to turn into ovens. We used to put books, bags, and portable fire extinguishers in the windows, so that we could keep them open. Once, during a lecture, a foam-based fire extinguisher was knocked down from the windowsill by the strong gust of wind. It landed on its tip, and sprayed vast amounts of white foam over the screaming, fleeing students. I still recall the faces of the cleaning staff, when they saw what the lecture hall turned into.

Priorities, of course, did matter in that new Romania... Heating was not as important as the installation, at an enormous cost, a tiny private TV station on the top floor of the building that was partly owned by the University... It failed to obtain a broadcast licence, but it swallowed huge funds - while thousands of students were freezing in their double jumpers and coats in the very same building.

This was, just a few years after the changes, a very accurate and small-scale illustration of the ways in which the entire country used to operate. The top priority was the making of quick profit, without any long-term business plan or any consideration for the human costs.

Our generation had been loudly proclaimed after the Revolution as *the* generation that will build the new world. Certainly, the diabolical decline in canteen food quantity and quality was among the things that made us feel very valued... There were no real economic reasons for this; simply put, the educational system has plummeted to the bottom of the neo-communist Governments' priority list; they have been too busy with robbing the country blind.

The army was serving better food than what we used to find in our canteen. This situation was completely reversed when compared to the reality under Ceausescu. The food was truly dire and it came in small portions; we were hungry just a couple of hours after lunch... Whenever trucks filled with cabbages arrived at the canteen kitchen, we knew: we were in for a few months of cabbage soups, to be followed by mashed cabbages and some tiny meaty bits - until the stock terminally rotted in the cellars, or it ran out. We used to bring sandwiches to the lectures; buying snack food all the time was simply out of the question due to the escalating prices.

The white-hot Revolutionary zeal in us had cooled like some slowing lava flow; still, there was some *naiveté* left in us... Many of us had thought that by 1995, the year of our graduation, the world around us would be vastly different compared to the one that we had kicked onto the pages of history books in those last few days of 1989...

Of course, reality kicked in during the last few months of our studies, just before the final exams. It became obvious that, in a country where surreally corrupt and self-centred new elite had occupied all layers of political and economic power, nothing had really changed.

We were able to think, say, and write anything – finally; but corruption, frustration, and disillusionment had replaced all our post-1989 utopian visions.

XX. ETHER

The hunger for moments of beauty, compelling people to seek out either magical sounds or imagery, has not changed in us after the paradigm shifts of post-Revolution Romania. Many music and film fans have kept their healthy addictions; in the "new world", myriad sources of sounds and images have become available.

Proper copyright laws did not exist yet in Romania. Mountains of pirated audio and video cassettes, imported mainly from Poland, were being sold – and they were selling like hot bread. When I began to write serialised essays on electronic and progressive rock music, my articles immediately found editors who were willing to publish them. One of these editors, with his ears attuned to the new expressions of old needs, later moved on to radio broadcasting. He dragged me into an unfamiliar, mythical, but utterly fascinating world of sonically insulated, and badly ventilated, cubicles of wood and glass. These had scary, large microphones, and clumsy headsets that weighed a ton. We recorded there several series of thirty-minute shows about music, films, and film soundtrack – he, always in a state of passionate professionalism, and I, always in a state of total, but restrained, amateurish excitement.

Every recording session, which used to last, on average, about an hour and twenty minutes in the case of a thirty-minute programme, was an adventure. First, there was the non-trivial task of catching two different buses and a tram to get to the studio after lectures. Then the real thrill of recording came, of transforming thoughts into magnetised particles on age-old reel-to-reel tapes.

Unlike that state-owned radio station, the private FM radio stations were turning up like mushrooms in the 1990s; the latter were invariably equipped with state-of-the-art computerised gizmos, and they were able to broadcast a mixture of adverts and music tracks without human intervention - often, without human soul...

We, in the old AM radio studio, used reel-to-reel tape recorders that literally had the size of domestic washing machines. They looked like something Noah had used to record messages that summoned the animals. These were waist-high metal boxes, which were able to propel tapes at a speed of 38 centimetres per second. This meant a superb sound recording and reproduction quality in those analogue days. The sound technician woman, who assisted the recording sessions, used to struggle with old valve amplifiers and intermittent connections, with cables that came loose half-way through a phrase or a piece of music. Then she had to stop the tape, find the place where it all went to pot, re-record, cut, splice with admirable precision and dexterity... She had to fade in and out manually, balancing many sliders, achieving a seamless transition that listeners were happy with...

Each such interruption caused by sometimes human, and often technical, problems was costing us many long minutes; so our sessions sometimes took entire afternoons, if we boldly attempted to record several episodes of the series. I remember that we were physically exhausted by the time we finished, especially as I did not possess the professional routine that would have enabled me to take all that mayhem into my stride. As I could not glide over the technological bumps with ease, the latter often affected my mind and, eventually, my voice.

Still, it was highly educational to learn how to edit an interview - not with a computer, but with a pair of scissors and sticky tape. We used to perform a very odd-looking routine: manually spun the reels, listened to wobbly alien voices that were speeding up and slowing down, found the exact point to cut the tape at – then came the cutting, the splicing, the combining, and the throwing away... I used to stand in the middle of a growing mess at my feet, a plastic chaos of tape pieces of various lengths.

Due to the lack of brand new magnetic tapes, these fragments used to be joined together in order to form a longer usable tape, possibly a few minutes' worth. We were borrowing from each other such chunks of tape, and used to collate these with sticky tape. It was an exercise in relativistic time; we were stretching, shrinking time, while we were fragmenting, and re-assembling tape under our fingers. Sound quality, especially where the tapes were joined together, used to degrade quite rapidly - and eventually the tapes, assembled from fragments, had to be thrown away.

Our greatest regret came from the fact that, with all this re-using and recycling of our prime material, namely those measly magnetic tapes, many recordings of radios shows were lost forever. Very rarely, special interviews made it into the so-called golden archive.

I wondered what Stockhausen or other early pioneers of electronic music would have thought, if they saw our truly post-modern, but organised chaos of magnetic tape fragments. Voices, noises, musical notes and textures were becoming one piece of tape that preserved new sounds for a while, before it was again cut up and assembled in some other way. Pieces and sounds were re-organised into something new for a while, then we recorded over them – and pushed the previous strange concoction of sounds into oblivion.

All those articles and shows could have become parts of a mere self-gratification exercise - an act of writing and then reading something about my passions, the sounds and images that had haunted me in the most pleasing ways since my early teens. However, as it turned out after the first few shows had been beamed into the distance by our antennae, it was not the case. Listeners devoured the sounds, wrote in, and phoned in, asked questions, asked for more, asked how they could get their hands on the music and the films we talked about...

In a moment of passion, I had also the initially stupid-sounding idea of setting up a music club, where people would come once a week to listen to previously unavailable music. They would listen to mostly unknown pieces that existed on my bookshelves, thanks to other music fanatics who had allowed me access to their rare collections of sonic wonders.

The local, and newly established, youth organisation in my hometown was very receptive to the idea; they put me in contact with the Dean of the local Unitarian church. Well, various figures of the RMDSZ (the Democratic Association of Hungarians in Romania) were approached first, because their office building had some huge meeting rooms - but they were already beyond the point of offering anything concrete to the local community.

Thus, a charming old man, who sat in his cosy, but modest, office in the Unitarian church, listened to my hopelessly timid explanation of what I had imagined. Let people come, for free, to evenings of music, and my friends and I would bring the some sound equipment. The speakers would come from one friend, the amplifier from another, the cassette player from me and various people on a rotational basis.

He said yes. The local newspaper agreed to print the adverts for each session. The council room of the church, to my immense joy, used to fill up with people who were hungry for music. I always read a few things about the artists and the music we were about to listen to, then the "stage" was handed over to the cassette player. During the following few years, we managed to treat our audience to sounds from my and others' music collection. We even had guest speakers; there was also interest from the local press and radio, so we created a few "spin-off" shows and articles with selected music. I used to specialise in electronic music, space rock, progressive rock, world music, fusions of genres and styles...

It may have seemed like some oddball "new age" gesture, but we often turned off the lights, and we put just one candle on top of the amplifier placed in the middle of the table. Abstract, otherworldly pieces, like the ones composed by the electronic music genius Klaus Schulze, had visible effects on the audience - people used to drift into a state of quiet wonder. I recall the effect of albums like Schulze's *Timewind*; when we turned on the lights after the hour-long session, there was a dazed silence for almost twenty seconds – and then, as if we had actually performed something, there was deafening applause in the council room. Kudos to those visionary musicians, who were being gradually discovered by many music fans only after the collapse of the Iron Curtain. To us, if I am honest, of course it felt great. We managed to take the audience on a journey; for many it was the first such journey they have been on – our only contribution was passion, a pair of speakers, a cassette player and our painstakingly assembled music collections that we had built over several years.

In that world of the Romanian '90s, copyright was still an abstract concept. We were exploiting that legal void, indeed - but not with the aim of making money; we just let people listen to works that they may have only heard about, to music that they discovered in that room for the first time. I knew all too well, what it felt like to be knocked out by a piece of music, and then to have to spend sometimes years with the search for a poor quality cassette copy of it.

Amidst the CDs and DVDs that fill my shelves now, all easily acquired in vast music stores or via some clicks in online shops, those years of passionate needing and wanting seem downright bizarre...

However, I recognise in the people who used to flock to our musical evenings the same hunger that had made me embark on long bus journeys to the home of a collector I had met during my years spent at University. I had been going through his collection; we had been discussing and comparing, listening and commenting... I had belonged to a wonderful network of utterly passionate and selfless people. All of them had gone to great mental, physical, and financial lengths in order to get their hands on wonderful music.

The mental image of some sad geek, who was sitting in a room stuffed with collected and beloved objects, is as far from reality as possible. These people had been sharing their treasures, which they had accumulated over many years of needing, wanting, and tediously acquiring… and I remain forever grateful to those wonderful music fans.

XXI. EVOLUTION

Eighteen years after the Revolution, a national survey asked the part of the Romanian population, which had memories of the totalitarian regime. Only 10% of the subjects felt that their lives improved after the Revolution...

Thus, the measurement of progress is an odd thing. Whatever tools one uses to measure it, the picture can look radically different if one changes a reference point...

There was huge "progress" made in spiritual matters, for example. Salman Rushdie's *The Satanic Verses*, with great delay, was eventually published in Romanian language, too. This, in isolation, could have been considered laudable progress. However, the Romanian Orthodox Church promptly published a statement that condemned the book's publication. Several TV channels fumingly quoted the fact that Rushdie had been sentenced to death by Ayatollah Khomeini because of this very book - as if the latter fact could have somehow justified the condemnation coming from a very different Church.

It was truly amazing to see Khomeini being quoted in 2007, in the mass media of a democratic and enlightened European nation. The minor facts that the death sentence had been lifted, and that Rushdie had come out of many years of hiding, were omitted by the Romanian Church.

There is "progress" in historical and political thinking, too. As mentioned earlier, in 2006 a national survey conducted by the main Romanian national TV channel TVR1 has shown that on the list of the Top 100 great Romanians, the fascist dictator Ion Antonescu was in 6th place. Ion Codreanu, the founder and key figure of the fascist Iron Guard that assassinated even high-profile writers, was also on the list, in the 22nd place.

All progress in a society is enabled, supported and driven by how that society educates its people. Many journalists in the UK have written eloquently about the British education system. It has been widely publicised, that British sixteen-year-olds have deplorable literacy and numeracy skills, while they still pass with flying colour the tests they had been trained to pass.

In this sense, Romania is well aligned to even the UK... Most secondary and high school students have developed repulsion toward real learning. Their system of values centres on the rights they have (and the absolute lack of responsibilities), on their material things (one is measured by which iPod model he/she has, not by the ability of being able to even read), and their status on various internet social networks. They, especially kids of the *nouveau riche*, have been constantly, and loudly, stating their various rights – without any sense of responsibility.

Since the Revolution, the Romanian education system has successfully evolved to reach the same dubious standards one finds in the previously so elusive West. Pupils graduate high school with appalling literacy and numeracy abilities, with shocking lack of general knowledge, a total ignorance of even their own, let alone world, literature and history.

The 2008 baccalaureates managed to beat all previous years' records in Romania in terms of corruption. More than fifty identical Romanian literature exam papers were found in just Bucharest alone. It all pointed to a wonderful and well-organised underground business of replicating and selling the exam subjects' solutions. They had even bribed teachers to close a blind eye to the whole thing... In 2014, not much has changed; in just one county, hundreds of baccalaureate diplomas were issued by an official, who specified his price in advance.

The exam results in recent years have been abysmal. The national statistics on the pass rates have even become the subject of creative YouTube videos that have gone viral. The Romanian education system, in which it is possible to see an education minister changed five times in just nine months, is tragicomic. However, this may become less of a "problem", as baccalaureate diplomas have been abolished at the end of 2014 as mandatory elements of the University entrance examinations.

Chaos has remained at the centre of that system. I vividly recall my last days at University, in 1995. On the day before our final exams, we had been waiting on the corridors, hoping to find out about the rumoured changes in exam regulations. Some exams were rumoured to have been added, but nobody knew whether those were to be mandatory for our diplomas or not. Mutually contradicting faxes had been arriving from Bucharest, and in the end, our lecturers and we had decided to turn up in the morning of the first exam and to play it by ear. We actually sat through the first exam, not knowing whether it is needed or not... It was – but this information only got confirmed later on.

Such tragicomic farces have very much remained the norm... In 2008, the theology students at Cluj have found out just six days before their final exams that they had to do an extra year of studies. In 2013, just two weeks before the start of the school year, parents did not know yet whether their children would start the newly introduced "zero year" in school, or they would continue in kindergarten for another year.

Sometimes, the entire structure of the school year, including the start dates and the holidays, was shuffled around just a few days before the school was supposed to start. In 2013, the authorities delayed the school start by a week, and then they suddenly changed the dates back – so the heads of kids, parents, and teachers were, by then, spinning faster than that absurd funfair ride. The entire textbook for the med school entrance exams of 2014 were changed halfway through the academic year at the end of 2013.

"Education, education, education" was the exact mantra used by both Ceausescu and Tony Blair. Interesting how they ended up in the same sentence; the essence of the mantra and the political intent was the same, just the context was entirely different.

While one leader, a demented dictator, had been treating the education system as a brainwashing tool, the other leader saw education as something that constantly needed to be raised to new heights. Ironically, in both cases the kids suffered the most - because as soon as education is reduced to mere political strategy, the kids become the least important elements in the equation. Everything in education, in both countries, had become just a mass of data that was endlessly analysed, ranked, and compared.

The Romanian education system has not gone backwards, as some may claim, it has actually evolved. In the UK, the GCSE results have been constantly amazing – increasing number of pupils pass with countless A and A* marks, but even basic general knowledge, literacy and numeracy skills have plummeted to shameful levels. SAT examinations for school kids were recommended to be abolished, because of the "stress levels" that they cause… One has to wonder about the sensory thresholds that we want kids to have, and their readiness for real challenges in life…

In a world, where some banal toothpaste can "amaze" you (to quote the advert slogan), but there is a continuous threat from germs to unhealthy food to terrorism, one has to wonder: where are our current sensory thresholds set to? After all, while we are so desperately coming up with new ways of protecting ourselves from "stress", we are cultivating fear and paranoia. A leading brand of surface cleaner does not just clean nowadays – it "protects you and your family", again to quote the advert, because it kills 99.9% of germs… Even its primary feature has changed into something that openly emphasises (and thus sells) fear.

In order to reduce "stress" and "difficulty", clearly we must destroy more and more of our education system. Studying Shakespeare even from modern English transcriptions and "summarised" text is too difficult; thus, we now show video highlights of the Bard's plays during literature lessons. Reading is tiring, it was said to be also stressful (!) for kids. Physical education classes are too demanding; thirteen hours of lectures and seminars per week are intolerable at for University students - the list of high-profile "problems" could go on forever. What kind of people are we actually producing in such education systems? What are we preparing them for?

While exam results have been getting better each year, the level of general and specialised knowledge has gone through the floor in every single survey done in the past years, because we are trying to "protect" the kids. Nobody speaks of different *kinds* of stress. Stress is a mantra now, over-used by teachers, parents, and the Government. It is a buzzword, a huge canvas, onto which many negative psychological scenarios can be painted - as if being tested in school is something that would mark school kids for life.

If one manages to establish a society where basic general knowledge is virtually absent, then one creates a perfect society for *selling* anything. One can watch with great amusement how myriad useless products can actually be sold in vast quantities, simply because most customers cannot spot the marketing nonsense that often contradicts basic biology, chemistry, or physics...

Many adverts, in order to get past the regulatory bodies, have pushed language to its very limits. Something is not sold because it has a certain effect – it is sold because, as the advert states, science *suggests* (instead of *proves*) that the product *may help* with *some* factor that *seems* to lead to the stated effect. The actual meaning of such statements is... zero, when it comes to actual claims on measurable and *proven* effects. One just has to *believe* in the product.

We do need, of course, a small minority of people who have the brains, who went to proper schools, and who passed proper exams with proper marks. They can develop such products, or at least they are able to invent the marketing slogans that avoid the risk of scientific or legal challenge.

There is no crisis of faith. Many may have lost their "traditional" and well-established faith, but they have acquired new belief systems. These have been rapidly elevated to the level of new orthodoxies and dogmas – and those, inevitably, bring with them a form of soft fascism.

One such orthodoxy is, of course, the saving of the planet. Aside from the scientific battle, and the correct or incorrect arguments in the debate, this orthodoxy is a hugely successful and enormous marketing engine. Any product that has run out of steam resurfaces with renewed vibrancy (at least in terms of its marketing), with newly acquired planet saving potential. Even the humble washing up liquid is greener nowadays, because it comes in a more concentrated form, hence it takes fewer trucks to transport it... This is just one example of truly desperate, opportunistic, and convoluted hammering of a new message into something old and banal.

In the UK, the Labour Government had introduced a 5% compulsory bio fuel quota. A survey by Oxfam revealed however, that this quota had caused enormous harm to food production where it was the most needed; it had negatively affected the welfare of millions. It has led to the cutting of enormous areas of forests, because the latter have been replaced with plantations in order to produce crops for biofuel.

Parallels and contrasts can go on forever: the Earth Hour initiative vs. the long haul flights taken by its fountainhead while he was organising the first such event; or the green initiatives of the airline industry (carbon "offset" charges and so on) vs. airlines that have flown empty Boeing 747s, in order to avoid losing their airport slots...

We are establishing an eco-warrior soft fascism. It is a new creed, an absolute dogma even, while fundamental things that *actually* make a difference are left untouched – but at least we get people to focus on the size of the washing-up liquid bottle. Such dogmas sell very well.

It is just ironic for someone, who had been wearing double jumpers in unheated classrooms and residence halls, to hear save-the-planet slogans that instruct us to turn the down the heating in the house and put on an extra jumper. I just quote here the British media campaign... At a distance of more than two decades and fifteen hundred kilometres from the point in time and space where I was last told that reducing heating would save the world, it strikes me as tragicomic the way in which dogmas have come full circle – only the context has changed.

Health is another major obsession of the increasingly less and less educated masses. While Romania has been copying all the habits of the West (fast food and vast amounts of sugary drinks having been the first things to explode on the scene of the suddenly changed country), health-mania has also exploded in the everyday life. There is no problem in the latter *per se*; however, marketing tricks combined with the plummeting levels of education in schools provide the same tragicomedy as in the West that they copied so hastily.

We devour vitamin supplements, gazillion banal juices that are saturated with anti-oxidants proven *not* stop our cells from aging (only the cells of worms the initial study was based on). We prolong life by eating and drinking the myriad new concoctions sold at hefty prices. There are acres of vitamin pills in every supermarket, all shouting: prolong your life! Stay young!

Omega3 oils have absolutely no proven actual effect at all on IQ, but we buy Omega3-enriched bread that makes our kids more intelligent. Recent long-term study on vitamins showed that devouring often 10-50 times daily normal amounts of vitamin A & E actually reduce life expectancy and cause immune system problems. It just confirms common sense and knowledge of fifth grade biology.

Still, not many people change their shopping habits, and few stop buying cubic feet of pills that claim to prolong life.

Whatever science says, it just bounces off the teflon coating of ignorance mixed with successful propaganda that fuels non-factual, extremely biased, partial truth-based orthodoxies. So, at least in one area, Romania has truly reached the levels of Western culture... As Umberto Eco stated, we all have returned to a medieval society, a medieval mind; superstitions, pseudo-scientific wizardry, and various beliefs replace scientific facts. Latter are ignored when those do not confirm our subjective opinions about health, longevity or, ironically, higher intelligence.

Changes have of course occurred also in the West, societies have gone through remarkable (and not always positive) changes and shifts in their systems of values.

Britain, the historic citadel of modern democracy, has gone through changes that were as rapid and dizzying as some in the countries of the former communist block were. While the latter has been emerging from the dark tunnel of Stalinism, the former had been entering a tunnel – one that was terrifyingly familiar to those who had left a similar one not so long ago.

It was spine tingling to see Tony Blair's government introduce a ban on any demonstration within a radius of 1000 yards around the Parliament. It was chilling to see 1.1 million people demonstrating in London against the Iraq war – and even more chilling to see them being completely ignored by the Government.

It was eerie to hear about anti-terrorism laws that allowed police to hold people without any trial for extensive periods... just because some politicians had replaced the Cold War with the "War on Terror" against an enemy that is mostly faceless and globalised.

In Romania, we had and still have no photography signs around any "strategically important" buildings; the only change compared to the old signs is that these were replaced with a stylised picture of a more up-to-date SLR camera instead of the old pictogram...

In parallel, during the Tony Blair years, the UK has embarked on a truly Stalinist cult of paranoia – but in the name of the battle against terrorism. Indeed, there is a serious threat from terrorists of all kinds; however, the way in which this threat has been treated by the Government and the media was eerily similar to classic Stalinist propaganda tricks. We even had a poster campaign, which told the public to report, or even challenge, people with cameras if they looked or acted "suspicious".

As the countless high profile cases have shown in the press and in newsletters of professional photographers' organisations, British police had not only challenged, but also literally attacked and arrested perfectly innocent amateur and professional photographers. As it was reported by reputable organisations like the *Bureau of Freelance Photographers*, many members were subjected to classic abuses of power.

The "price is worth paying", as some Government officials had stated, when the scandals kept turning up in the mass media - and we *all* need to do "something". Even if "something" went against fundamental human rights. At least such phrasing has openly admitted that the "War on Terror" was, among other things, a perfect political manipulation tool; it helped to instate unprecedented levels of control, which could be felt if one just walked around taking snapshots of cities in London and elsewhere.

To induce mass paranoia about overblown and omnipresent dangers, to divert attention from real problems – these were classic Stalinist methods, very familiar to anyone who had lived in the communist block. To see this so openly strutted in a so-called "free country" was quite astounding. Not only that it was manipulative, it was very effective, too, judging from the number of police abuse cases that targeted members of the public. Amateur and highly respected professional photographers, even tourists had been at the receiving end of "anti-terror" measures.

Thankfully, as these excesses occurred in a still functioning country with checks and balances, the situations were resolved – but they remain spine chilling, nevertheless. The Chief Constable even had to issue further "guidance" notes to their staff, and photographic organisations issued cards to their members that explained to police officers the fundamental legal framework they must still respect.

In the 21st century, ordinary persons who took pictures of landmark buildings were treated as potential terrorists... In severe cases, it took days to resolve the situation – especially when the photographer, in full knowledge of still applicable laws and Constitutional rights, refused to be subjected to that treatment.

There was no real difference between the "no photography" signs of the Romanian communist past (plus the consequences of transgressions), and the so-called British Terrorism Act's infamous sections that had labelled any photographer as a potential threat to society. The only small difference had been the cause in the name of which the paranoia had been induced.

There was even a UK hotline number, which we could call - we could phone in with our suspicions. The culture of suspicion, and the culture of reporting people, was very familiar to us during the Ceausescu regime. The so-called War on Terror was, perhaps, *the* holy grail of some manipulative politicians. Apart from the genuine dangers, this so-called war was even more of a perfect mind-altering tool than what had been used during the Cold War.

Latter had had a somewhat geographically localised, and a reasonably clearly defined and identifiable, enemy. Of course, for someone like McCarthy it had meant a faceless and lurking enemy; anybody could have been a subversive element. For Ceausescu, enemies had been lurking everywhere - enemies of him, of his society, or enemies of the system.

During the Tony Blair years, while we were having contradicting or wildly different security measures at different airports within the same city (and across the EU), this new War was the ideal tool for Philip K. Dick-style manipulation of the collective psyche.

The enemy is not geographically localised, it is not limited to a particular ethnic group... It really is faceless, ubiquitous, and not localised in time either; its actions are not linked to a certain political system or regime. It, hence also the war against it, could go on forever...

Many of the Terrorism Act's sections that were haunted by Stalin's ghost have been promptly repealed by the following British Government. While there is a genuine threat, and there is continuous effort to combat it, the so-called free Western and Romanian societies have both continued to cultivate fear.

We used to have one clearly defined fear that permeated every day of our lives. Now, we have a plurality of fears – and we have the freedom to choose our fears. Fear of germs, with myriad banal household products that "protect us" constantly; a fear of accidents and lawsuits, with increasingly tragicomic health & safety and political correctness rules; fear of aging, of fading physical beauty, fear of finances... it is an almost endless list.

Mind the gap, mind the step, plastic bags are lethal if you put them on your head. Teakettles could get hot. Trampoline manufacturers have to warn parents not to install the product near metal railings as kids could bounce onto them and impale themselves, as it actually happened several times. Even basic parental and/or self-preservation instincts are being affected by the mass stupidity campaigns.

Romanian kids, on a school trip in Transylvania, asked the teacher why there were no warning signs near the cliffs' edges. The teachers often give up and no longer go on excursions, as kids can nearly kill themselves in situations that any sane person with some common sense, and intact self-preservation instinct, would avoid or resolve easily.

We have been creating a new kind of person. What had happened during a Bakerloo line power cut in the London underground system makes one wonder: was our basic, fundamental instinct replaced with a total reliance on warning messages, guidance notes, and legal disclaimers? The irony, as it happened then, is that overblown health & safety rules actually backfire completely; furthermore, people, who find themselves millimetrically outside their everyday routine, can completely lose themselves in a situation that can be easily dealt with. Reliance on one's own common sense is no longer necessary. We have endless lists of rules, invented by bureaucrats, and those solve everything for us.

It seems, at least in Britain, that around 60% of surveyed parents no longer dare to let their kids get farther than 100 yards from the house. The reason, quoted invariably by exponents of this "free" society, is danger. We live in a very dangerous world nowadays - so it seems. The slight problem is that statistics do not support such deep-rooted feelings about the omnipresent so-called dangers. The survey had had the same result even in very safe, very good neighbourhoods. Our "reality" has never been so threatening… or so it seems.

Media, of course, has been playing a key role in building this warped perception.

Another study, where kids were GPS tagged, revealed the obvious. The kids who were not on a short leash, who were not escorted by adults and "protected" all the time against absolutely everything, happened to roam, explore, interact more with objects, places and people… The net benefits are very clear to anybody who did not grow up in a society that was continuously stunned into a state of panic and fear of everything.

Intuitive intelligence is decreasing every day in the societies of both my former and current home. We are becoming, with amazing speed and effectiveness, a thoroughly stupid and incapable race. As long as we can function in our own world, constructed around monotonous routines, and in the bubble of consumer goods and rules that "protect" us, we can feel comfortable. Monsters are lurking beyond the walls of our houses. We are back to the frame of mind of the medieval Man.

A landmark ruling by the High Court in 2008 has taken the UK a step closer to an "informant society", one along the lines of the former East Germany or Soviet Union. Someone was fired from his job when an enhanced criminal record background (CRB) check turned up allegations of abuse. He took his case to a judicial review, arguing that the allegations were seriously flawed and unsubstantiated, and that the police should have only included them in a CRB check if the allegations had been believable at least. This view was rejected, as a judge ruled that the actions of the police were acceptable; in addition, future employers should be aware of the allegations, however weak and subjective they had been.

For those who had seen the real experts in such matters during the 50s-60s-70s-80s in the Eastern Block, all this sounded perhaps too familiar. If one just changed the names and the context, the entire case sounded like a straightforward case of informants' unsubstantiated allegations that led to one's life having been ruined – basically, one was guilty until proven innocent.

Hungarian ethnic minority in Romania was labelled, both before and after the Revolution, subversive and dangerous. The scare tactics are the same, just context and key words differ. How do the electoral campaigns run by the extreme right in Romania differ from the tactics used in British newspapers about immigration and related issues? How does the scaremongering done by Romanian xenophobes differ from British nationalist propaganda? Familiar headlines shout continuously about immigrants overloading and ruining the British education system, health service, and transport system... Everything that does not work in this country is the fault of immigrants.

As a Hungarian ethnic, I am used to hearing how everything was and is our fault in the pre- and post-Revolution Romania. Now in the UK I am hearing how immigrants are generally the root cause of the disgraceful state of social infrastructure, health, education, transport, well, everything really.

The same emotions are exploited with irrational headlines and with partial truths. Coupled with an exponentially intensifying dumbing down of society and societies, such propaganda keeps finding most fertile soil. The UK

Independence Party exploits perfectly the xenophobia, on individual and national level.

Extreme views are easy to trigger and nurture, in lack of proper education about the fundamentals of the subject areas targeted by the media and politicians.

If one does not know any fundamental biology, then one only eats fat-free yogurt because one believes that any amount of any fat is bad for the body, or at least it makes one fat – never mind the several times higher sugar content... If one has no idea about history, economics and politics, one believes everything any extremist journalist or politician throws at one. The former leader of the British National Party talked about "white indigenous English population"; on hearing this, anyone who knew just a tiny amount about the history of Great Britain laughed him- or herself to the remote control and changed the TV channel.

Benevolent-looking extremism has never been so omnipresent and effective as it is in today's Romania and UK. Being able to draw such parallels is something one could not have predicted two and a half decades ago.

XXII. CHOICE

One possible option after I finished University was to stay there as an assistant lecturer; not much else was on the horizon for me in the field of electronics or software. The other option was to spend three years in the UK on a PhD project that was to have practical applications. It was to be funded by an EU contract, and offered me a chance to undertake research into artificial intelligence.

The prelude to this was the Tempus program, which allowed a few students to spend their last semester at a University abroad, whilst they were finalising their diploma project. The selection of the students and their choice of a certain University were supposed to be done based on points achieved in specific exams. However, in reality the selection, like everything else in Romania, was heavily based on the classic who-knows-who method.

The deputy dean of the Faculty, who was managing the local aspects of the Tempus program, tried to get one of his protégés to the UK. The lad achieved only third place during the competition for the student placements. Still, promptly after the December competition, he was secretly lined up for the top place, namely the UK placement. Once the typical manoeuvre was found out, as much as possible scandal was stirred up. It then took us until February next year to get the rules of the Tempus program finally enforced, via firm instructions from the French Tempus manager...

After that typical corrupt mess, I finally obtained what was due - and departed to the UK, to spend three months at a research centre. This was collaborating with the nearby University, and both institutions wished to embark on a thrilling EU-funded project. During my final weeks there, I received an invitation to return there, once I get my diploma, with the purpose of working on a PhD project.

Naturally, I considered the obvious differences between the possibilities offered in the UK and in Romania - it really was a no-brainer. Did I really want to go back to a Romanian University that was still engulfed in power struggles and continuous power abuse by certain staff?

Entire student projects were being copied into books published by certain lecturers; the real authors were not credited, and there was no possibility for a student to demand this. My entire third year signal processing project had ended up as a chapter in one of the books published by a lecturer. First and second year students used to spend long afternoons with the editing of such books, which were collated from student projects and foreign publications. Those students-turned-typists had been promised good marks at exams, but nobody gave a damn about those who were the authors of those chapters. Latter even received threats from the respective lecturers...

For me, the choice made in 1995 felt like a clash between my personal interests and the larger picture... It was a choice between a life in which, besides obvious benefits, one did not feel like a third-rate citizen - and a life in which, besides the economic and professional shortcomings, the myriad everyday immoralities made one feel queasy.

It is a bizarre feeling not to have a real home, in its widest sense - an unconditional, permanent, and stable one. Transylvania feels like home, as long as one does not have to interact with the new Romanian ultra-corrupt "elite", or with the new and freely flaunted chauvinism directed against any ethnic minority.

In Hungary, the Transylvanian immigrants are not exactly liked – they have been accused of driving salaries down and "stealing" jobs from the locals; standard xenophobe rhetoric, really. Again, not exactly a home... even if it is sometimes called "mother country".

In the UK, I am of course one of the naturalised immigrants who have been listening to the discourse of various parties about immigration. It was quite a pleasure to have the word "alien" used as a label for us; I still have somewhere my old green "Alien Registration Certificate". Although I have been a subject of the Queen for more than ten years, the reality still is that I am on an island, amongst people who still keep a very insular outlook on the world despite the current realities of that world.

I have become a tourist in my homeland. I fly home, gypsy kids spot me from miles away, as I am a "wealthy" foreigner. They offer to carry my suitcase, and they are extremely insistent; thus, I experience the guilt-generating duality. On one hand, I know very well that they really *are* desperately poor, but I never let them anywhere near my stuff.

I look out for older taxi drivers who are touting at the airport, I analyse their intonation, their accent, I check whether they speak a more educated Romanian or not... I try to find clues, via both rational and utterly subjective means, about what social category they belong to, so that I can feel safer from being ripped off. However, it is impossible for me to do all this with the nonchalance and the superiority of a foreign tourist.

I am from, and *of*, that land; I had spent there many years dreaming – not about wealth, but mere normality, not abundance, but mere decent sufficiency... An unexpected turn of fate had given me qualifications, experience, and money, oh yes, money. J.L. Borges wrote that money is the most abstract thing - because it only represents *possibilities*; it is up to one how one spends it, and what one spends it on...

My homeland has seen poverty on a scale that has only vaguely been sketched by the BBC documentaries and exploitative shots of the "exoticism" of rural Romania, with its orphans and street kids. That land still makes me think twice whether I *need* something or not – and this always comes before the *want*.

Thus, in many ways, and no matter how odd it sounds, I am grateful for my first, almost nineteen, years of my life that I had spent in all possible kinds of darkness. However, this feeling is not the perverse, and partially amnesiac, nostalgia of the many Romanians who think it was better under the old regime.

The almost two decades that I had spent under a totalitarian regime have made me appreciate the small things in life, in the absence of anything else. In a society where perfect paranoia had meant life-saving awareness, "them" was not a paranoid delusional term, but a tangible reality that one wished to avoid at all costs. Hence, one had learnt how to see through most kinds of manipulation.

Those years had taught me that I could only rely on myself. They had taught me: after I had been repeatedly knocked to the ground by the daily reality, my only choice was to pick myself up and carry on - cautiously, but with determination. Otherwise, the regime would have won. Those years also enabled me to look at things from an often-unusual viewpoint. They made me able to see some parallels, even disturbing ones, between a world that had defined my childhood and adolescence, and another world that is trying to define the rest of my adult life.

I used to think that certain facets of society were confined to certain geographic areas and historic periods. However, it was quite a learning experience to realise that many of those facets are actually universal.

Gordon Brown had been talking about someone's idea of placing hidden listening devices in lampposts, just to augment our War on Terror… Here we are, those darn ears again.

It does not matter *why* myriad ears are placed around us, the essence of *what* those mean for basic human liberties remains the same. During Tony Blair's government, one could do a simple search and replace on certain words in the statements that were emanating from 10 Downing Street... One could then easily realise that merely context, time, and space have changed since eerily similar measures, thoughts, and speeches were thought up by other, more dubious, leaders – no matter how benevolent the central arguments seemed on the surface.

On the quantitative side of things, everything changed... We want more, as we have more choice; sometimes infinitely more, if we believe what is stated on posters, the covers of books, CDs and DVDs that inundate every minute of our lives. I am not really complaining; my own recollections of how I had spent years with the hunt for a copy of some music in the Romanian 70s-80s seem surreal to me. Now - a few clicks on Amazon, and... tada...

Umberto Eco wrote eloquently about the ways in which we use "more" as a term. Do we really have *more*? Every new film that is released has automatically at least four stars on the posters. It is automatically "film of the year" (even in January...), "instant classic", "unmissable", it is a "must see". One month later, nobody remembers those utterly forgettable films.

We are desperately exaggerating our mundane lives, because we need to feel that our banal monotony is somehow special. The London Underground status reports always show "good service" when trains just about manage to run on schedule. Normal service is *not* something special, and it does not have the extra sweetness of "good". It is merely normal.

Our sensory thresholds and our expectations have been drastically lowered.

We, to quote Eco's astute observations, no longer say "another coffee please", we say "*more* coffee please". The newsreaders before a commercial break do not say "we continue after the break", they say "more to come after the break".

While Eastern Europe is still unconditionally copying everything that is Western, it is also striving for individuality. It does the latter with great desperation. All the "tribes" that emerged in the West exist back home, too – the goths, the emos, the rockers, and so on. They are essentially clusters of identically dressed people with identical hairdos and makeup – while they are trying to be individuals…

A well-known jeans manufacturer had been advertising a particular model of jeans with a slogan that shouted, "Be individual". The contradiction, although deafeningly loud, was not strong enough to have made the tens of millions of customers, who bought those identical pairs of jeans, notice it. However, such self-contradicting slogans exist in identical way in the East, too.

Unfortunately, real soul, real quality, or real goodness is only present as a trace element on the streets. Hence, every publisher, media mogul, designer, and marketing guru is inundating our senses with the overblown and extraordinarily ordinary flood of desperately hyped quality, value, goodness in the widest sense. They are trying to convince themselves, and us, that what they are selling us is not utterly forgettable, soulless, and brain-numbing most of the time.

In true post-modern fashion, we are turning lack of value into value, absence of signs into signs, lack of content into not just content, but unmissable and must-see, must-hear, must-consume content… The lack of meaning that tries to increase our perception of, or even belief in, increased values and content does not only turn up in advertising and the world of consumer goods. A slogan in a high-tech company had recently conveyed to its employees the strategic objectives of the department they worked in; a main objective was to become "the coolest software execution environment in the industry". Yes, it is a literal quote. It would be impossible for any strategist and/or corporate communications manager to define the word "cool" in the context of measurable things.

It is a society where, on the surface, the Nanny State (as it was called in the UK) takes care of every thought, aspect, step, diet, sight and sound, just to make one's existence as *comfortable* as possible... It makes the majority of people downright incapable of thinking for themselves, of making real choices.

The fundamental mistake made by the former communist dictators had been the creation of sharp contradictions between reality and dogma, between words and tangible facts. The ideal totalitarian regime, though, is the one depicted by Philip K. Dick's *The Mold of Yancy*; in that world, there is total freedom of expression and total freedom of thought, but everyone is gently steered toward the same thought patterns, same opinions and choices... They *could* choose many different paths, ideas, products... but they do not. While exactly such a transformation is occurring in Eastern Europe, one does wonder how some Balkan countries can apply the EU regulations.

While driving through rural areas of Romania, one can see eloquent examples of just how impossible it is to apply EU agricultural norms there. The age-old tradition of slaughtering pigs in winter, of processing the meat and the entrails at home, is still going strong. Huge rural areas of Romania are still stuck in the 12th century. People, who had been living in mud huts, were moved by Ceausescu into blocks of flats... but they only knew one way of life. Thus, many had ripped up the floorboards in their new flats, and then planted vegetables in a few inches of soil that they had brought in from somewhere...

At street level, how and when will such backward mentalities change? People throw litter out from the upper floors of the blocks of flats, although there are garbage shuts; even in the country's capital, one can see rat-infested garbage piles growing between the buildings. When will the desire for a civilised existence be triggered in such people? Such trivial, and taken-for-granted, elements of everyday "civilised" life need to be instated first, before anybody even dreams of properly enforced laws or regulations.

Romania is still the land of paradoxes. The signing of some EU papers was just the start of a long process that is still in its embryonic state, despite almost a decade having elapsed since.

Every visit to Romania, while I immerse myself in the reality I no longer belong to, throws me into a schizoid state of mind; maybe it is more accurate to say schizoid state of soul... That reality is saturated with simultaneous disillusionment and hope, with astounding opposite extremes of deep poverty and stratospheric wealth. Many people welcome one with a smile, and they unconditionally, as we say, would sell the skin on their back just to be able to truly welcome and treat the visitor... However, plenty of others welcome one with a fake smile, and dangerous ambitions fired up by one's relative wealth...

Every single day, streets are filled by people who still cannot bring themselves to dishonest ways of making money; but other streets can only be frequented safely by the people who never made an honest dime in their life, and never will... It is interesting to notice small details; for instance, what proportion of people who drive the flashiest cars are seriously rough-looking underworld characters? One can get angry at the sight of the new "elite", which, with few exceptions, is composed of truly primitive, amoral, and ultra-corrupt people. They invariably have zero knowledge about, or appreciation for, the values of the spaces they inhabit, and they drive the latter literally to ruin. Old palaces, restaurants with illustrious past and luscious interiors have fallen into a state of ruin, as the *Golden Cockerel* has in my hometown. Alternatively, in lucky cases, such priceless architectural gems have been turned into bingo salons or hotels.

Heavy mists of anger also descend on me, when I watch the new self-obsessed cliques of power being incapable of using the riches of that land for economic benefits... They are very good at exploiting the resources for their *private* purposes, but not for building wealth in, and for, the country. Some flashy resorts near the Black Sea are charging exorbitant prices, for a level and quality of services that are deplorable by Western standards – except the areas essentially reserved for the "elite". Many people find it cheaper and infinitely more civilised to drive down to Bulgaria, where the more restrained greed and better business attitude have created superb resorts with very normal price schemes.

The Romanian businessmen and politicians who are in charge of tourism, or are part of that industry, have the Danube Delta, the Black Sea, countless mountains resorts of astounding beauty, but all in desperate need of modernisation. They have volcanic lakes, geothermal phenomena like Lake Sovata, which is unique in Europe. They have countless naturally sparkling mineral water sources with proven medical benefits. There are rivers and lakes for fishing and relaxation... Come on, modernise those resorts properly, and exploit, in the good sense of the word, your treasures; bring in the crowds of tourists that used to flock to Romania in the '70s and '80s...

Instead, apart from turning a few ski and Black Sea resorts into havens for the closed circles of power for their own debauchery, most resorts are falling apart, metaphorically and literally. Casinos are built, while castles and palaces crumble. Illegal hunting, fishing, and tree cutting goes on and on, while beauty disintegrates and falls into such an unsound state, that even major tour operators had to remove certain Romanian destinations from their lists of package holidays.

Sixteen years after the Revolution, international tour operators like TUI had actively discouraged tourists to go to the Black Sea. In the meantime, other countries like Bulgaria and Croatia have become tourist havens; clearly, there is something special about the Romanian ultra-corrupt, totally egocentric, and power-drunk "high society". The last time the Romanian government organised an international propaganda campaign to get tourism going, the politicians spent tens of millions of euros... and ended up almost dragged to court, as even the logo of their horrid marketing material was plagiarised.

So yes, I do get angry whenever that country, hijacked by its new and utterly destructive elite, is regressing into a state that has not been seen since the WW2. Behind the façade, there is a struggling nation, which has been trying to find again its moral compass. The people still doubt whether it is worth finding it, whether morals have a place at all in that world. For many, principles and a system of values are just ballast, which would be slowing them down in the process of making a quick buck.

I get angry at first, whenever I enter a shop and the sales people look at me as if I had exterminated their families. Often I am not angry with them, but with the system and with their employers. Those employees often work twelve hours per day, six days a week, for a revolting pay – so, 25 years after the changes, they still cannot see a customer as a valued person. In their mind, there is a complete disconnect between a customer feeling good, the profits that the shop may make, and the employees' rewarding – as there seldom is any reward of any kind.

However, despite all of this, whenever I go back home I still feel that I am going *home* - and I could not, would not, imagine myself dying in a foreign land... However, at the same time, I cannot imagine myself *live* in my homeland.

No aristocracy had started with wealth acquired via honest and/or moral means... It took them time to turn themselves gradually into nobility, after generations and generations of exploitation, killing, conquering and stealing. Romania's old and ennobled aristocracy had fled when the communists came; some returned after the end of the regime, reclaimed some of their properties. Most of them, though, stayed away from that land that has been trying to find its way among too many and too sudden possibilities, among too many ghosts.

Nostalgia does exist, as surveys showed that people still remember fondly the dictator. A taxi driver told me that the terrible traffic problems in my hometown should be solved with the clear thinking that the dictator had had. We have too many cars nowadays, so either we demolish these large historic buildings, or we introduce the rule that only cars with odd and even registration plates can be on the streets on odd and even days, respectively...

People squeezed by inflation, by huge prices, by the alignment of energy prices to European prices, and by the financial or employment uncertainties tend to forget the sinister side of the former dictatorship. They would trade in, without one moment of doubt, personal freedoms for some sort of desperately wanted stability – even if that stability came with total moral destruction.

In England, there was a case of a cemetery's administrator, who had knocked down old headstones; his motivations were in the sphere of health and safety-related paranoia. A society that knocks down its own headstones and vandalises its own graveyards is highly symbolic in every respect. In Romania, according to surveys, it seems that people are ready to vandalise or to erase their past, to invent a new history; they are even ready to bring back old ghosts, in order to restore some sense of order to their seemingly chaotic and uncontrollable world.

Still, I wonder whether I really wish those people to evolve towards what the fervent imitation of the West will bring into their lives. I wonder whether they will need "mind the step" warnings at the bottom of every staircase; whether they will bend their own language out of shape to avoid any gender-specific verbal constructs so that they can always be politically correct.

I wonder whether they will use dozens of chemicals on every surface of their homes, just to sterilise those against the lethal germs the adverts warn them about all the time; whether they will irreversibly exchange their glorious cuisine for a diet of burgers and vitamin supplements... Obesity statistics have already skyrocketed, because in just two decades, Romania has successfully copied the dietary habits, especially the fast food culture and sugar overload, of the West.

I wonder whether they, too, will end up substituting the genuine freedom of thought that they had fought for with something that only resembles freedom on the surface; whether, in actual reality, the vast majority will be driven and manipulated towards having virtually the same thoughts, opinions, and tastes... This transformation is well under way already, because now they are faced with countless choices in everything, instead of the former confinements of simple dilemmas during the past regime.

While they feel torn between the myriad novel possibilities, and, at the same time, they are crushed by economic realities, they are rapidly forgetting – and they are forgetting to pass their memories on to the younger generations. A survey conducted on the 18th anniversary of the Revolution had targeted 18-year-olds; it showed that vast majority of them had no idea even of what had happened to Ceausescu. The question was simple: did he resign or was he removed from power…

It is a society without an even remotely accurate past - we only need to think of Daicoviciu's theories that have been shaping the collective psyche for several generations. It is a society lives so desperately in the present that it puts even the always-rushing West to shame… It still faces huge challenges; it is still fighting with many ghosts that masquerade as new flesh-and-blood beings… If one reads Ray Bradbury's *The Haunting of the New*, well, it can be seen as a wonderful allegory to what is happening at home, my real home.

I just hope that they will remember something about a previous, quite rudimentary, existence; I hope that they can teach their kids about life on a level that is somewhere between two extremes – between the humble simplicities of the past, and the unconditional copying of the West. I hope that those valleys, hills, and plains will be inhabited by people who will regain their *true* identities – people, who will be free (and, above all, will be able) to make genuine choices in their lives.

After that society's still ongoing post-traumatic stress syndrome caused by the vast changes fades, then maybe the faces one can see on the streets nowadays, those overworked, blasé, and disillusioned faces, will change.

I hope that then they will be again lit up with self-confidence; I hope that they will have many reasons to smile again at each other - and even at the stranger that I have become.

ABOUT THE AUTHOR

Lehel Vandor (1971-) was born in Transylvania, and grew up, as a member of the Hungarian ethnic minority there, during Nicolae Ceausescu's totalitarian regime. His school, and later high school, studies have been completed during the communist dictatorship.

The 1989 revolution in Romania and the 1990 ethnic pogrom organized by the newly formed Romanian extreme right happened during his final year at high school. In 1990, the first generation of students of the free Romanian began their University studies. Lehel Vandor, too was among them, and the five years of student life have been a memorable experience in the country that was just starting to find its way.

After finishing University in Transylvania, he obtained his PhD in the United Kingdom and permanently settled there. Radical changes in British politics, 9/11, the subsequent War on Terror, and its measures introduced by Tony Blair's government have provided numerous opportunities for drawing certain disturbing and surprising parallels between two very different societies caught up in their ideological and political fights with very different enemies.

Previously Lehel Vandor authored several series of articles and radio programs in Hungarian and Romanian languages, published short stories in Hungarian language. His photography is represented by several photo libraries. One of his other passions is electronic music composition and production.

Made in the USA
Charleston, SC
20 October 2014